Rehabilitation
Institute of
Chicago
PROCEDURE
MANUAL

CLINICAL
MANAGEMENT
OF RIGHT HEMISPHERE
DYSFUNCTION

Martha S. Burns, Ph.D., CCC-SP

Anita S. Halper, M.A., CCC-SP

Shelley I. Mogil, M.S., CCC-SP

AN ASPEN PUBLICATION®
Aspen Systems Corporation
Rockville, Maryland
Royal Tunbridge Wells
1985

Library of Congress Cataloging in Publication Data

Burns, Martha S.
  Clinical management of right hemisphere dysfunction.

  (Rehabilitation Institute of Chicago procedure manual)
  "An Aspen publication."
  Includes bibliographies and index.
  1. Communicative disorders. 2. Brain damage—Complications and
sequelae. 3. Cerebral dominance. 4. Brain—Localization of functions.
I. Halper, Anita S. II. Mogil, Shelley I. III. Rehabilitation Institute of
Chicago. IV. Title V. Series. [DNLM: 1. Brain Damage, Chronic—
complications—handbooks. 2. Brain Damage, Chronic—therapy—
handbooks. 3. Communicative Disorders—etiology—handbooks. 4.
Dominance, Cerebral—handbooks. WL 39 B967c]
  RC423.B86   1985   616.8   85-6217
  ISBN 0-87189-101-8

Editorial Services: M. Eileen Higgins

Burns, Halper, Mogil:

RIC Evaluation of Communication Problems in
Right Hemisphere Dysfunction (RICE)

Additional test booklets are available in packets of 25
copies.

1 - 9 packets	$19.00 each
10 or more packets	$17.10 each

Test packets are not returnable. Payment is due in U.S.
dollars. Maryland and California orders add state sales tax.

To order, send check or purchase order to:
      Aspen Systems Corporation
      P.O. Box 6018
      Gaithersburg, Maryland 20877

Library of Congress Catalog Card Number: 85-6217
ISBN: 0-87189-101-8

Printed in the United States of America

2   3   4   5

Table of Contents

Unit 5—Treatment of Communication Problems in Right Hemisphere Damage 57
Martha S. Burns, Ph.D., CCC-SP, Anita S. Halper, M.A., CCC-SP, and
Shelley I. Mogil, M.S., CCC-SP

Unit 6—Working with Families 97
Mary C. Kozy, A.C.S.W., and Gloria A. Tarvin, A.C.S.W.

Concluding Comments 105
Martha S. Burns, Ph.D., CCC-SP

Contributors

MARTHA S. BURNS, PH.D., CCC-SP
  Associate Professor
  Department of Communicative Disorders
  Northern Illinois University

JEFFREY L. CUMMINGS, M.D.
  Director, Neurobehavior Unit
  West Los Angeles VAMC (Brentwood Division)
  Assistant Professor of Neurology in Residence
  UCLA School of Medicine

ANITA S. HALPER, M.A., CCC-SP
  Director, Department of Communicative Disorders
  Rehabilitation Institute of Chicago
  Associate, Department of Rehabilitation Medicine
  Northwestern University Medical School

MARY C. KOZY, A.C.S.W.
  Clinical Social Worker
  Rehabilitation Institute of Chicago

SHELLEY I. MOGIL, M.S., CCC-SP
  Clinical Supervisor
  Department of Communicative Disorders
  Rehabilitation Institute of Chicago

GLORIA A. TARVIN, A.C.S.W.
  Director of Social Work
  Rehabilitation Institute of Chicago

Preface

So intense has been the attention paid to the function of the right hemisphere in recent years that one can begin to sense the excitement that must have accompanied Broca's and Wernicke's revelations about the aphasias over a century ago. The interest is much broader now, since so many behavioral disciplines have evolved in recent years. Professionals in the fields of psychology, linguistics, speech/language pathology, social work, and neurology share a bond with the patient with right hemisphere damage in their efforts to better understand the constellation of cognitive disturbances that comprise the syndrome.

To the clinical scientist falls the burden of effective rehabilitation of the patient with right hemisphere damage. As most soon discover, this burden can be overwhelming and can quickly quell the enthusiasm generated from theoretical speculation. These patients are real persons, men and women who once led productive lives but are now thrust into a world that apparently looks and feels very different from the world that their integrated brain perceived. What is worse, as we are only now beginning to realize, is that as a function of the same disturbance the patient with right hemisphere damage is unable to communicate despair or confusion effectively to others. The result is that this patient is easily cast aside as an uninterested or uncooperative partner in the rehabilitation team. Thus, although written for the clinician, it is to the patients with right hemisphere damage that this book is dedicated. Our goal has been to provide a comprehensive yet practical compendium for effective management of these patients by all professionals who must deal with the cognitive components of the disease.

Clinical Management of Right Hemisphere Dysfunction grew out of a manual developed to teach clinical management of patients with right hemisphere damage. It has been organized into three general sections. The first provides three units that review the neurological and psychological research on right hemispheric processing. In Units 1 and 2 Cummings summarizes the medical literature on the role of the right versus left hemisphere and the effects of unilateral brain damage. In Unit 1 he provides a perspective on the historical evolution of our current concepts, and in Unit 2 he reviews many common and rare right hemisphere syndromes with attention to localization.

In Unit 3 Burns summarizes the neuropsychological and neurolinguistic research on lateralization of cognitive functions as well as provides a review of current linguistic theory on pragmatics of communication. She then integrates the two bodies of literature to propose mechanisms for understanding the range of communication disorders observed in these patients.

In Units 4 and 5 Burns, Halper, and Mogil present clinical methodologies for diagnosis and treatment of patients with right hemisphere damage. Research reviews are used as a departure point for generating a practical approach to the clinically relevant components of right hemisphere dysfunction.

Tarvin and Kozy, in Unit 6, present the social implications of brain damage and provide practical approaches for reintegrating the patient back into productive personal life.

It is our hope that all rehabilitation scientists who must contend with the real effects of brain damage on a human's world will find this book a helpful and encouraging addition to their clinical library.

Hemispheric Specialization: A History of Current Concepts*

Jeffrey L. Cummings, M.D.

Development of the current understanding of hemispheric specialization can be divided into three historical eras. The first era concerned the discovery of dominance of the left hemisphere for language. Paul Broca was a principal figure in this initial historical finding. The second era involved explaining the role of the white matter tracts that connect areas within the same hemisphere and that provide connections between the two hemispheres. The major contributors in this period were Roger Sperry and Norman Geschwind. In the third era there was a rapid expansion of knowledge regarding the functions of the right hemisphere. This most recent period has restored a balanced view of the roles of each of the hemispheres, with both making distinctive contributions to the ecology of human intellectual activity. These periods in the evolution of the knowledge of hemispheric specialization, along with an overview of the functions of the two cerebral hemispheres, will be presented in this unit.

PAUL BROCA AND THE DOMINANCE OF THE LEFT HEMISPHERE

Broca's discovery of the dominance of the left hemisphere for language was anticipated by localizationist theories that were proffered early in the 19th century.

The most well known of these early concepts were promulgated by Franz Joseph Gall and his student Johann Gaspar Spurzheim, who fostered a school of thought known as phrenology and maintained that mental functions were able to be localized in the brain. They further contended that the relative development of mental functions resulted in deformations of the overlying skull such that an individual's abilities could be determined simply by palpating the shape of the cranium.[1] The latter idea enjoyed great popularity among the lay public but was ridiculed by the scientific community and gradually lost favor in the early 1800s. Although Gall was an accomplished anatomist and his ideas presaged many contemporary concepts of hemispheric specialization, his association with phrenology led others to link the concepts together and to deprecate theories of cerebral localization.

After Gall's death in 1828, J. B. Bouillaud, among others, continued to champion the concept of functional localization within the hemispheres, but major and enduring support for an association between localized brain regions and specific neuropsychological activities came only with the discoveries of Paul Broca.[2,3] In 1861, Broca, a French physician and anthropologist, reported two cases of aphasia associated with left-sided frontal lobe lesions. Two years later, he described the autopsy results of eight patients with aphasia and noted that all lesions involved the third frontal convolution on the left.[4,5] This momen-

*This project was supported by the Veterans Administration. Norene Hiekel prepared the manuscript.

2 CLINICAL MANAGEMENT OF RIGHT HEMISPHERE DYSFUNCTION

tous observation provided the basis for all future investigation of hemispheric specialization. Broca appears to have realized the profundity of his discovery when he stated, ''and, a most remarkable thing, in all of these patients the lesion existed on the left side. I do not dare to draw a conclusion and I await new facts.''[4] Confirmatory findings were not long in coming, and a special role for the left hemisphere in language function was soon firmly established.

Carl Wernicke made the next important observation regarding the dominance of the left hemisphere for linguistic abilities. At the age of 26, Wernicke published a small monograph on aphasia in which he described for the first time sensory aphasia and discussed the importance of the fibers connecting the posterior temporal with the inferior frontal regions of the left hemisphere.[1] In addition to refining understanding of the role of the left cerebral hemisphere in the mediation of language, Wernicke's discoveries also contributed to the growing impression that the left hemisphere was dominant for many and perhaps most intellectual functions.

This belief in the general dominance of the left hemisphere was further encouraged by Hugo Liepmann, who published his paper describing the apraxias in 1900.[1] Liepmann observed that apraxia was more common with left-sided than with right-sided lesions, thus providing support for the major role of the left hemisphere in certain motor activities as well as in language function.

Despite occasional observations to the contrary, the view of the left cerebral hemisphere as dominant for most intellectual functions was endorsed from the late 19th century to the mid 20th century. Indeed, animals were thought to have the equivalent of two right hemispheres, and the human's phylogenetic supremacy was attributed solely to the accomplishments made possible by his dominant left hemisphere.[6] This lopsided view of cerebral function was challenged by descriptions of behavioral deficits following focal right-sided damage, but major advances in reforming the concepts of a general left hemisphere dominance awaited discoveries concerning the role of white matter tracts providing intrahemispheric and interhemispheric connections.

DISCONNECTION SYNDROMES AND THE SPLIT BRAIN

The role of the corpus callosum and of the white matter of the brain had long remained an enigma.

Galen, in the second century AD, postulated that thoughts were generated in the cerebral ventricles and saw no role for the corpus callosum, and, in 1664, Thomas Willis suggested that the callosum was the seat of the imagination. Felix Vicq d'Azyr, a French anatomist and personal physician to Marie Antoinette, held the first modern view of the function of the corpus callosum. In 1784, he suggested that ''the commissures are intended to establish sympathetic communications between different parts of the brain, just as the nerves do between different organs and the brain itself.''[7]

The first clinical syndromes attributed to disruption of the corpus callosum were described by Joseph Jules Dejerine and Hugo Liepmann. Dejerine, in 1892, described a patient who suddenly developed a right homonymous hemianopia along with an inability to read. Paradoxically, the patient retained the capacity to write in spite of the inability to read his own writing. The patient died and at autopsy was found to have a lesion in the left occipital region and the posterior aspect of the corpus callosum. Dejerine postulated that the syndrome reflected the blindness of the right visual field (produced by the left occipital lesion) and an inability to transfer visual information from the intact right hemisphere to the left hemispheric language areas through the damaged corpus callosum.[8] The callosal lesion thus disrupted transfer of information from the right to the left hemisphere and produced the specific clinical syndrome of alexia without agraphia.

As noted previously, Liepmann had an intense interest in the apraxias, and, in 1907, Liepmann and Maas discovered that a lesion of the corpus callosum resulted in an isolated apraxia involving the left arm and leg.[7] The callosal lesion prevented the transfer of impulses from the left to the right hemisphere for control of the left-sided extremities.

Unfortunately, these early insights into the function of the corpus callosum and the syndromes that result from callosal injury were largely ignored, and the role of the callosum in coordinating the activities of the two hemispheres was lost to investigators succeeding Dejerine and Liepmann. Thus, in the 1930s and 1940s, when Akelaitis and colleagues examined patients with partial or complete sections of the callosum performed for control of epileptic seizures, they were unable to identify any persisting deficits.[7] These observations led inevitably to the conclusion that the corpus callosum played no major role in cerebral function.

This view was challenged by experimental observations made by Ronald Myers and Roger Sperry at the

University of Chicago. They found that when the optic chiasm of a cat was severed and the animal was trained with one eye patched, intraocular transfer of information occurred, and the cat performed normally when using the untrained eye alone. If both the chiasm and the corpus callosum were sectioned, however, such transfer of information did not occur. The results implied that the corpus callosum was responsible for transferring the visual information from one hemisphere to the other and that surgical sectioning of the callosum disrupts this normal flow of information.[9,10] These experiments prepared the way for the rediscovery of the role of the corpus callosum in humans.

One of the first modern descriptions of deficits resulting from damage to the corpus callosum in a patient was reported by Norman Geschwind and Edith Kaplan in 1964.[11] They studied a patient who suffered an anterior cerebral artery occlusion with infarction of the anterior portion of the corpus callosum. His deficits included aphasic agraphia when writing with the left hand but not while writing with the right; impaired object identification and tactile letter naming with the left hand but not with the right; and apraxia of the left hand but not of the right. Each of these abnormalities reflects the inability to transfer information between the two hemispheres through the damaged corpus callosum. Aphasic agraphia of the left hand results from the inability to transfer linguistic output from the left to the right hemisphere, which controls the left hand. Left hand anomia is similarly a product of the inability to transfer tactile information, as is unilateral apraxia a product of the inability to transfer a motor command. Following these seminal observations, Geschwind[12] described a series of clinical syndromes resulting from interruption of the corpus callosum or of white matter tracts within the hemispheres. His disconnection hypothesis provided both an explanation of many clinical observations as well as a conceptual framework for understanding the role of white matter tracts in integrating cerebral function.

A more complete explanation of the function of the corpus callosum, the deficits following transection of the callosum, and the abilities of the isolated right hemisphere followed the many observations made by Roger Sperry and his students and colleagues at the California Institute of Technology. They investigated epileptic patients submitted to corpus callosectomy by Joseph Bogen and Philip Vogel for control of epilepsy. These ''split brain'' studies corroborated and extended the observations of Geschwind[12] and of Geschwind and Kaplan.[11] The most startling and dramatic revelations of these experiments concerned the diversity and sophistication of neuropsychological capabilities of the right hemisphere, the degree of independent mental activity demonstrable in the disconnected right hemisphere, and the differences in cognitive styles exhibited by the left and right hemispheres. The callosal syndrome described by Liepmann and later by Geschwind and Kaplan[11] was confirmed in the commissurotomized patients. In addition, it was shown that the disconnected right hemisphere possessed at least rudimentary skills for auditory and written language comprehension, that it mediated highly developed visuospatial skills, and that it could provide the basis for a sophisticated emotional and mental life previously considered unique to the language-dominant hemisphere. The discoveries resulting from the study of the commissurotomized patients culminated in the award of the Nobel Prize in Medicine to Dr. Sperry in 1982.

HEMISPHERIC SPECIALIZATION AND THE FUNCTIONS OF THE RIGHT CEREBRAL HEMISPHERE

In 1874 in an essay entitled ''On the Nature of the Duality of the Brain,'' John Hughlings Jackson first proposed that the two cerebral hemispheres had different functional roles.[13] He hypothesized that the left hemisphere was responsible primarily for mediating verbal activity, whereas the right was devoted to the ''revival of images in the recognition of objects, places, persons, etc.'' This view anticipated many contemporary ideas concerning the respective functions of the two halves of the brain, but they gained little currency until the split-brain observations offered new support for their validity.

A list of functions attributable to each cerebral hemisphere is presented in Table 1–1. The list is derived from observations of patients with lateralized brain damage (see Unit 2), from studies of split-brain patients in which surgical interruption of the corpus callosum allowed the functions of the two hemispheres to be studied independently, and from experimental investigations involving normal subjects in which auditory dichotic or visual high-speed tachistoscopic presentations of stimulus material reveal statistical preferences for processing by one hemisphere. Such studies demonstrate that both hemispheres participate in most intellectual activities but make separate contributions to the final cognitive accomplishments.

TABLE 1–1   Principal Functions of the Two Cerebral Hemispheres

	Left Hemisphere	Right Hemisphere
Language	Speaking aloud	Auditory comprehension
	Auditory comprehension	Reading comprehension
	Naming	Prosodic expression
	Reading comprehension	Prosodic comprehension
	Reading aloud	
	Writing	
Constructions	Internal detail	External configurations
Calculation	Arithmetic processing	Spatial arrangement
Memory	Verbal	Visuospatial
Miscellaneous	Praxis	Facial recognition

Language functions are mediated predominantly by the left hemisphere, but the right hemisphere has significant linguistic communication. (See Unit 3 for a detailed discussion of right versus left hemispheric communication skills.)

Constructional deficits, although often considered indicative of right hemisphere damage, are approximately equally likely with lesions of either hemisphere.[14] This suggests that both hemispheres make essential contributions to this visuospatial ability. The two hemispheres, however, each aid the constructional process by providing different types of input.[15,16] The right hemisphere appears to be most involved with providing external details and general orientation and the left hemisphere with contributing essential analysis of internal details.

Calculation, like constructional and linguistic abilities, requires the activities of both hemispheres and can be disturbed by lesions of either. Left hemisphere damage results in an impairment of mathematical symbolization, whereas right hemisphere injury produces disturbances in visuospatial organization of the digits.[17]

Each hemisphere also mediates different aspects of memory. The left hemisphere is essential for verbal memory abilities; the right hemisphere is responsible for nonverbal memory skills.[18]

A few abilities appear to be mediated primarily by one or the other hemisphere. Praxis, the ability to perform learned skilled movements, is dependent on left hemisphere integrity,[19] whereas the right hemisphere has superior skills for recognition and matching of facial expressions.[20]

Thus, each cerebral hemisphere is specialized for the accomplishment of specific tasks or of specific aspects of functions performed in common with the contralateral cerebral member. The right hemisphere, formerly relegated to an inferior role and considered capable of only an animal-like level of intellectual performance, is now believed to make essential contributions to many intellectual abilities. The dominance of the left hemisphere for many propositional aspects of language is unchallenged, but the right hemisphere is no longer considered with the ''minor hemisphere'' and is itself dominant for many intellectual functions.

THE SEARCH FOR ORGANIZATIONAL PRINCIPLES

The demonstration that the two hemispheres are performing complementary but different tasks has led to a search for a single dimension, the two poles of which would represent the function of each of the hemispheres. A list of the dichotomies that have been proposed is presented in Table 1–2.[21–23] Most of the dichotomies emphasize the verbal-linguistic-propositional functions of the left hemisphere and the nonverbal-visuospatial-emotional functions of the right hemisphere. Although such dichotomies are true in a general sense, the investigations reviewed previously

TABLE 1–2   Dichotomies Proposed to Characterize the Functions of the Two Cerebral Hemispheres

Left Hemisphere	Right Hemisphere
Verbal	Nonverbal, visuospatial, preverbal
Linguistic	Visual or kinesthetic
Expression	Perception
Auditoarticulary	Retino-ocular
Symbolic or propositional	Visual or imaginative
Propositioning	Visual imagery
Executive	Storage
Relations	Correlates
Logical, analytic	Holistic, synthetic
Propositional	Appositional
Serial	Parallel
Focal, discrete	Diffuse
Difference detecting	Similarity detecting
Time dependent	Time independent
Segmental	Spatial, global

Source: Adapted from Bogen JE: The other side of the brain. II. An appositional mind. *Bull Los Angeles Neurol Soc* 1969;34:135–162; from Bradshaw JL, Nettleton NC: The nature of hemispheric specialization in man. *Behav Brain Sci* 1981;4:51–91; and Bryden MP: Laterality: Functional Asymmetry in the Intact Brain. New York, Academic Press, 1982.

have shown that the right hemisphere has considerable linguistic abilities and the left hemisphere makes essential contributions to visuospatial functions. More broadly encompassing dichotomies have been proposed by Bogen,[21] who suggested that the left hemisphere operates in a propositional mode whereas the right hemisphere has appositional characteristics, and Semmes,[24] who hypothesized that the left hemisphere is organized in a more discretely localized manner whereas right hemispheric organization is more diffuse. Each of these approaches identifies important differences between the functions of the left and right hemispheres, but none is sufficiently inclusive to embrace all neuropsychological abilities of each of the hemispheres. Indeed, it seems unlikely that the two hemispheres are precisely complementary. Each hemisphere has unique capacities and functions but acts in concert with the other under normal circumstances, and each produces a unique pattern of deficits and preserved abilities when damaged.

REFERENCES

1. Eggert GH: *Wernicke's Works on Aphasia: A Sourcebook and Review*. The Hague, Mouton Publishers, 1977.

2. Duffy CJ: The legacy of association cortex. *Neurology* 1984;34:192–197.

3. Geschwind N: The organization of language and the brain. *Science* 1970;170:940–944.

4. Joynt RJ, Benton AL: The memoir of Marc Dax on aphasia. *Neurology* 1964;14:851–854.

5. Schiller F: *Paul Broca*. Los Angeles, University of California Press, 1979.

6. Smith A: Dominant and nondominant hemispherectomy, in Kinsbourne M, Smith WL (eds): *Hemispheric Disconnection and Cerebral Function*. Springfield, Ill, Charles C Thomas, 1974, pp 5–33.

7. Joynt RJ: The corpus callosum: History of thought regarding its function, in Kinsbourne M, Smith WL (eds): *Hemispheric Disconnection and Cerebral Function*. Springfield, Ill, Charles C Thomas, 1974, pp 117–125.

8. Benson DF: The third alexia. *Arch Neurol* 1977;34:327–331.

9. Gazzaniga MS, LeDoux JE: *The Integrated Mind*. New York, Plenum Press, 1978.

10. Sperry RW: Cerebral organization and behavior. *Science* 1961;133:1749–1757.

11. Geschwind N, Kaplan E: A human cerebral deconnection syndrome. *Neurology* 1962;12:675–685.

12. Geschwind N: Disconnection syndromes in animals and man. *Brain* 1965;88:237–294, 585–644.

13. Jackson JH: On the nature of the duality of the brain, in Taylor J (ed): *Selected writings of John Hughlings Jackson*, London, Hodder and Stoughton, 1982, vol 2, pp 129–145.

14. Brown JW: Rethinking the right hemisphere, in Perecman E (ed): *Cognitive Processing in the Right Hemisphere*. New York, Academic Press, 1983, pp 41–53.

15. Gianotti G, Tiacci C: Patterns of drawing disability in right and left hemispheric patients. *Neuropsychologia* 1970;8:379–384.

16. Warrington EK, James M, Kinsbourne M: Drawing disability in relation to laterality of cerebral lesion. *Brain* 1966; 89:53–82.

17. Levin HS: The acalculias, in Heilman KM, Valenstein E (eds): *Clinical Neuropsychology*. New York, Oxford University Press, 1979, pp 128–140.

18. Butters N: Amnestic disorders, in Heilman KM, Valenstein E (eds): *Clinical Neuropsychology*. New York, Oxford University Press, 1979, pp 439–474.

19. Geschwind N: The apraxias: Neural mechanisms of disorders of learned movements. *Am Sci* 1975;63:188–195.

20. Ellis HD: The role of the right hemisphere in face perception, in Young AW (ed): *Functions of the Right Cerebral Hemisphere*. New York, Academic Press, 1983, pp 33–64.

21. Bogen JE: The other side of the brain. II: An appositional mind. *Bull Los Angeles Neurol Soc* 1969;34:135–162.

22. Bradshaw JL, Nettleton NC: The nature of hemispheric specialization in man. *Behav Brain Sci* 1981;4:51–91.

23. Bryden MP: *Laterality: Functional Asymmetry in the Intact Brain*. New York, Academic Press, 1982.

24. Semmes J: Hemispheric specialization: A possible clue to mechanism. *Neuropsychologia* 1968;6:11–26.

Neurological Syndromes Associated with Right Hemisphere Damage

Jeffrey L. Cummings, M.D.

Damage to the right hemisphere results in some of the most bizarre and complex syndromes observed in clinical medicine. Visual hallucinations, denial of illness, unilateral neglect, amnesia for nonverbal material, and loss of speech prosody are among the unusual symptoms exhibited by patients with injuries lateralized to the right side of the brain. In the initial part of this unit, the anatomical and biochemical differences between the two hemispheres will be presented. After reviewing these distinguishing physical features, the clinical syndromes resulting from unilateral right hemisphere damage will be presented.

ANATOMICAL AND BIOCHEMICAL DIFFERENCES BETWEEN THE HEMISPHERES

The two hemispheres have been known to differ functionally since 1861 when Paul Broca noted that left-sided lesions produced aphasia whereas right hemisphere lesions did not (see Unit 1). Despite this obvious functional difference, however, the two hemispheres were considered to be structurally identical until the seminal anatomical observations of Norman Geschwind and Walter Levitsky in 1968.[1] By systematically exposing the superior surface of the temporal lobe, they discovered that the planum temporale (the posterior area behind Heschl's gyrus) is larger on the left in 65% of brains and larger on the right in only

11%. Thus, the region of the brain crucially involved with language in the left hemisphere was consistently larger than in the contralateral hemisphere.

These original observations have been confirmed and expanded by other investigators. Gross anatomical asymmetries between the hemispheres include the configuration of the sylvian fissures, the size of the cerebral ventricles, the overall shape of the cerebral hemispheres, the volume of the anterior speech region, and the mode of crossing of the pyramidal tracts at their decussation in the medulla (Table 2–1).[2] The sylvian fissure divides the temporal lobe from the overlying frontal lobe. On the left, the fissure continues smoothly posteriorly, whereas the right angulates superiorly in the posterior region. This anatomical divergence is visible at autopsy and can also be identified on angiograms demonstrating the course of the cerebral vessels that lie within the sylvian fissures. The different positioning of the right and left sylvian fissures creates a larger planum temporale on the left and a larger inferior parietal region on the right.[3,4]

Pneumoencephalograms and computed tomography of the head reveal asymmetries in the cerebral ventricles. Between 60% and 75% of individuals have larger left-sided lateral ventricles. The width of the body and temporal horn of the left lateral ventricle is larger than the right, and the left occipital horn is longer.[5]

Asymmetries also exist for the anterior speech regions (Broca's area) between the left and right hemi-

TABLE 2–1   Anatomical and Biochemical Differences Between the Left and Right Hemispheres

	Characteristic	Hemisphere Asymmetry
Gross Anatomy	Planum temporale	Larger on the left
	Anterior language area	Larger on the left
	Hemisphere shape	Longer and wider in left occipital lobe and right frontal lobe
	Sylvian fissures	Extend more posteriorly on the left and more superiorly on the right
	Lateral ventricles	Body and temporal horn wider on the left, occipital horn longer on the left
	Pyramidal tract	Larger left pyramidal tract crosses above the right in the medullary decussation
Histology (Cytoarchitectonics)	Planum temporale	Larger histologic area on the left
	Posterior thalamus	Larger on the left
	Auditory thalamus	Larger on the right
Biochemistry	Acetyltransferase	More concentrated in left temporal lobe
	Norepinephrine	More concentrated in left posterior nuclei and right somatosensory nuclei
	γ-Aminobutyric acid	Greater concentrations in left thalamus and caudate nucleus and right substantia nigra, superior colliculus, and nucleus accumbens

spheres. Although the exterior portions of the regions are of equal size, when the intrasulcal surfaces are also included a significant interhemispheric difference emerges, with the left side larger than the right.[6]

The two hemispheres are of different shapes. In a majority of brains the left hemisphere has a longer and wider occipitoparietal area and the right hemisphere has a longer frontal lobe. These asymmetries are determined by measuring the indentations made on the internal surface of the skull by the underlying brain (as revealed by computed tomography) and correlate well with the hemispheric asymmetries found at autopsy.[7-9]

The descending pyramidal tracts cross at the level of the medullary decussation. It is this decussation that underlies control of the right arm and leg by the left hemisphere and of the left arm and leg by the right hemisphere. This decussation is asymmetrical, with the fibers crossing from left to right doing so at a higher level in a majority of cases.[10]

The gross differences between the left and right hemispheres are visible in fetuses by 29 to 31 weeks' gestation and on endocasts of Neanderthal skulls that are 40,000 years old.[3,5,11-13] Similar, but less marked, differences occur in the brains of chimpanzees and orangutans.[14,15]

Histologic studies also reveal differences between the right and left hemispheres (see Table 2–1). Cytoarchitectonic investigations demonstrate that histologic

boundaries correspond to the gross asymmetries of the temporal lobes described previously.[2] Such studies also reveal that the thalamic nuclei (lateral posterior) projecting to larger left hemisphere regions are of correspondingly greater size and that those (medial geniculate) projecting to right-sided areas are increased in volume on the right.[16]

Biochemical asymmetries between the two hemispheres have received less attention and the results are less consistent (see Table 2–1). In humans, choline acetyltransferase concentrations are greater in the left temporal lobe than in the right.[17] The distribution of norepinephrine is more complex: its concentrations are greater in the posterior nuclei on the left and in the somatosensory nuclei on the right.[18] In the rat, concentrations of γ-aminobutyric acid are higher in the left thalamus and caudate nucleus and the right substantia nigra, superior colliculus, and nucleus accumbens.[19]

Thus, while being of overall similar size and shape, the two hemispheres harbor a variety of anatomical and biochemical differences. Most of the asymmetries involve regions of the brain concerned with language mediation and show a bias toward increased size of the left temporal and inferior frontal regions. The right posterior region, an area vitally concerned with visuospatial function, is larger on the right. In addition to the gross anatomical asymmetries, there are also interhemispheric differences in histologic structure and in the distribution of neurotransmitters. The asymmetries appear in the last trimester of gestation and were present in our Neanderthal ancestors.

CLINICAL SYNDROMES ASSOCIATED WITH RIGHT HEMISPHERE LESIONS

The neurobehavioral syndromes associated with lateralized right-sided lesions include visuoperceptual disorders, visuomotor abnormalities, affective alterations, memory disturbances, and neuropsychiatric disorders (see Exhibit 2–1).

Visuoperceptual and Related Disorders

Hemispatial Neglect

Hemispatial neglect refers to the failure of patients to detect, report, or orient to stimuli in one hemiuni-

---

Exhibit 2–1   Classification of Clinical Syndromes Associated with Right Hemisphere Lesions

Visuoperceptual and related disorders
   Hemispatial neglect
   Anosognosia
   Achromatopsia
   Environmental agnosia
   Facial recognition defects and prosopagnosia

Visuomotor disturbances
   Constructional disability
   Dressing disturbances

Affective and emotional alterations
   Aprosody
   Impaired affective auditory comprehension
   Disturbance of emotional facial recognition
   Altered emotional facial expression

Memory disorders
   Nonverbal amnesia
   Reduplicative paramnesia

Neuropsychiatric disorders
   Visual hallucinations
   Capgras' syndrome
   Secondary mania
   Acute confusional states
   Paranoid hallucinatory states

---

verse.[20] The neglected hemispace is contralateral to the lesion and occurs with parietal, frontal, and subcortical lesions, although it is most profound and enduring with parietal lobe damage.[21,22] Hemispatial neglect may follow damage to left-sided as well as right-sided structures but is more severe and persistent with right-sided damage.

Unilateral neglect manifests itself in a variety of ways. The patient may fail to attend to somatosensory, auditory, or visual stimuli on one side. When the deficit is mild, the neglect is evident only when both sides are stimulated simultaneously; in more profound cases, all lateralized stimuli go undetected. The patient fails to orient to stimuli originating in the neglected hemispace and may ignore or turn away from examiners approaching from the neglected side. When asked to copy figures, only one half of the model may be seen and reproduced, and when asked to cross lines distributed randomly on a page, the patient will cross only the lines in the nonneglected hemispace.[23] Hemialexia may result from reading only one half of words and sentences: "northwest" will be read as "west" and "baseball" as "ball."[24] Hemiacalculia may occur when only one half of a series of numbers is included in the calculation process. The patient will also perceive only one half of the environment and may become lost from missing all turns in the neglected hemispace.[25]

Hemispatial neglect tends to be most profound in the initial phase of acute right-sided lesions. The neglect may resolve over time but is commonly still detectable many months later.[26] Hemispatial neglect is independent of the existence of a visual field defect: patients with neglect may have no field defect, and patients with visual field deficits may have no hemispatial neglect.[27]

Anosognosia

Anosognosia refers to denial of illness and frequently occurs to some degree in patients with hemispatial neglect.[28] The most common form of anosognosia occurs with right parietal lesions and involves denial of contralateral hemiparesis, hemisensory loss, or visual field defect. The anosognosia varies from a simple underestimation of the degree of the deficit to a frank denial of any abnormality. In addition to denial of deficits, anosognosia also embraces a variety of unusual attitudes directed at the paretic limbs. Some patients minimize the deficits and joke about them (anosodiaphoria), some attribute ownership of the limbs to someone else (somatophrenia), some express hatred of the limb (misoplegia), and some exaggerate the strength of the limb (anosognosic overestimation).[29] A related phenomenon is the false belief that an additional limb has appeared on the paralyzed side.[30]

Anosognosia may constitute a considerable barrier to rehabilitation since the patient who is unaware of any deficit is unlikely to be successfully engaged in therapy.

Achromatopsia

Central achromatopsia refers to the loss of color vision produced by a brain lesion. It is limited to the hemifield contralateral to the lesion, and the necessary lesion is situated in the inferomedial occipital region anterior to the visual cortex.[31] Infarction in the distribution of the posterior cerebral artery is the most common cause of central achromatopsia, but the syndrome has been produced by brain tumors and other focal lesions involving the ventromedial occipital cortex.[32,33]

Environmental Agnosia

Environmental agnosia is a unique syndrome manifested by a loss of environmental familiarity and an inability to become topographically oriented even in familiar surroundings.[34,35] The patients are able to see and accurately describe the environment, and intellect and memory are unimpaired. Many develop verbal strategies to compensate for their recognition difficulties (e.g., "My bedroom is the third door on the left beyond the nurses' station").

The origin of the recognition deficit is controversial, with some investigators viewing it as an amnesia and others championing the idea that it is an agnosia.[36,37] In many cases, however, memory is intact, and patients with memory disturbances do not exhibit the syndrome. The deficit appears to result from an inability to match intact perceptions with completely or partially preserved memory stores. This matching process is necessary to allow recognition to occur and to impart a sense of familiarity to one's percepts. Thus, loss of environmental familiarity shares with other agnosias the essential feature of being a percept stripped of its meaning and is best classified as an environmental agnosia.

The lesion necessary to produce environmental agnosia is an inferomedial temporo-occipital lesion in the right hemisphere. Although most patients have had right posterior cerebral artery infarctions, the syndrome has occurred with other etiologies.[38]

Facial Recognition Defects and Prosopagnosia

Defects in the recognition of famous faces, of matching two identical faces from a series of similar faces, and of choosing a previously seen face from among a group of faces are all more common with right hemisphere lesions than with left hemisphere lesions and more common with posterior damage than with anterior damage.[39-41] Tests with split-brain patients suggest that the right hemisphere is normally superior to the left in encoding complex stimuli (such as faces) that cannot be adequately differentiated with a verbal description, and this skill is aborted by right hemisphere damage.[42]

Prosopagnosia is the failure to recognize familiar faces such as friends and members of one's own family. Recognition of familiar and unfamiliar faces depends on independent central nervous system mechanisms, and lesions may produce defects in one ability without impairing the other.[43] Prosopagnosia has usually been attributed to bilateral lesions of the posterior hemispheres, and all autopsied cases have had lesions of both hemispheres.[44,45] Prosopagnosia has occurred, however, in patients with computed tomographic evidence of unilateral right-sided lesions and in patients with unilateral surgical lesions, suggesting that appropriately placed lesions in the right hemisphere may be sufficient to disrupt the recognition of familiar as well as unfamiliar faces.[46,47]

Visuomotor Disorders

Constructional Disability

Constructional disability refers to the inability to draw spontaneously, copy model figures, reproduce geometric patterns with match sticks, or assemble blocks to imitate a model. There is a disturbance of assembling or articulating the parts that cannot be accounted for on the basis of visual, somatosensory, or motor deficits. Although often called constructional apraxia, the disability does not meet the definition of apraxia as an inability to perform on command an act that can be performed spontaneously.[48]

Unilateral lesions of either the right or left hemisphere may give rise to constructional disability, and the deficits are more profound with posterior than with anterior hemisphere lesions.[49-51] Qualitative differences between the drawings produced by patients with right hemisphere lesions and those produced by patients with left hemisphere lesions have been observed. Right hemisphere damage results in a tendency to neglect the left half of models, to make errors in spatial relations, and to overscore existing lines and add extraneous material. Patients with left hemisphere injury produce simplified drawings.[52-54] While consistently present, the differences between the drawings produced by patients with right and left hemisphere damage are not sufficiently distinctive to allow differentiation of lateralized lesions solely on the basis of the constructional product.

Dressing Disturbances

There are two types of dressing disturbances: one in which the patient suffers from severe unilateral neglect and fails to dress one half of his body, and one in which body–garment disorientation makes it impossible for the patient to align body and clothes correctly. In the latter the patient frequently turns the garment backwards or inside-out, inverts right and left or up and down, and is able to conquer the logistics of dressing only with great difficulty. Body–garment disorientation has a virtually unique association with right parietal lobe damage.[55]

Affective and Emotional Alterations

The right hemisphere has often been regarded as "the emotional hemisphere," mediating human emotional life. This hypothesis is too broad and is being progressively refined to determine which components of emotion depend on right hemisphere integrity. The experience of emotion is mediated by the limbic system, a system with bilateral representation. Expression of emotion in both voice and face and the perception of emotions in the voices and faces of others, however, are dependent on lateralized right hemisphere mechanisms. Among the emotional functions mediated by the right hemisphere are prosody of speech, affective auditory comprehension, recognition of emotional facial expressions, and emotional facial displays (see Unit 3).

Aprosody

Prosody refers to the affective coloring, melody, and cadence of speech. These nonverbal aspects of communication impart emotional content to propositional speech and allow communication of the intensity and variety of the speaker's emotional state. Normal prosody depends on both left and right hemispheric integrity, but right-sided lesions may impair prosody

without altering the propositional component of verbal output. Motor prosody is impaired by anteriorly placed lesions in the right hemisphere.[56-58]

Impaired Affective Auditory Comprehension

Comprehension of the affective or prosodic elements of speech is also dependent on the right hemisphere. Patients with right parietal lobe lesions fail to comprehend the prosodic speech elements but have no impairment of propositional language comprehension. Such patients also have difficulty repeating the affective intonation of sample sentences provided by the examiner.[59,60]

Disturbances of Emotional Facial Recognition

As noted previously, the right hemisphere is superior to the left on tasks of facial recognition and facial matching. It has been difficult to dissociate recognition of faces from recognition of facial expressions, but evidence is consistent in demonstrating that the patient with right hemisphere damage is disadvantaged in the recognition and interpretation of emotional expressions.[61]

Altered Emotional Facial Expression

Human emotions are expressed more intensely on the left side than on the right side of the face, suggesting an asymmetrical control of facial expression with a right-sided predominance.[62] Lateralized right-sided lesions are thus more likely than left-sided lesions to impair facial displays of emotional expression.

Memory Disorders

Nonverbal Amnesia

Right hemisphere lesions preferentially affect the recall of nonverbal visual material. Right temporal lobectomy results in impairment of retention of complex visual patterns and faces.[63] Right thalamic lesions also disrupt nonverbal memory in contrast to the impairment of verbal memory produced by left-sided temporal lobe and thalamic lesions.[64,65]

Reduplicative Paramnesia

Reduplicative paramnesia or environmental reduplication is a disorder of spatial orientation in which the patient insists that a current unfamiliar environment (the hospital) is located closer to a place that is more important and familiar (home).[66-68] The complex confabulation syndrome appears to depend on a combination of impaired spatial perception, poor visual memory, and an inability to recognize the dissonance in their responses. The patients have most commonly had a combination of right parietal and bilateral frontal injuries or right parietal damage and an acute confusional state.

Neuropsychiatric Disorders

Visual Hallucinations

Visual hallucinations can be operationally defined as a symptom in which the patient claims to see or behaves as if he sees something that the observer cannot see.[69] Visual hallucinations associated with lesions within the hemisphere may be ictal in origin, occurring as part of a focal seizure, or they may be "release" hallucinations associated with visual field defects. Release hallucinations are much more common with right-sided than with left-sided lesions and with lesions involving the posterior aspect of the hemisphere.[70,71] The hallucinatory visions tend to begin soon after an acute cerebral insult, occur in the region of a visual field defect, persist for several hours at a time, consist of formed images of animals or persons, and gradually abate after several months. The patient usually appreciates the hallucinatory nature of the images.

Palinopsia is a special variant of release hallucination in which the major feature is the abnormal persistence or recurrence of visual images after the exciting stimulus has been removed.[72] After looking away from the face or object, the original image persists for up to several minutes and may spontaneously recur several hours later. Palinopsia has the same association with lesions of the right posterior hemisphere that is noted with typical release hallucinations.[73,74]

Capgras' Syndrome

Capgras' syndrome is the delusional belief that individuals close to one have been replaced by impostors. The patient can detect no physical changes that distinguish the impostor but is convinced that an impersonation is occurring. Capgras' syndrome is often part of a complex persecutory delusion in which the patient believes that the impostor is perpetrating the masquerade in order to obtain money or property illegally.

Many patients with Capgras' syndrome have right hemisphere damage, and the syndrome has been observed in patients with post-traumatic encephalopathy, epilepsy, cerebrovascular disease, and a variety of other neurological disorders.[75-77]

Secondary Mania

Secondary mania refers to an elated and/or irritable mood lasting at least 1 week and combined with at least two of the following: hyperactivity, pressured speech, flight of ideas, grandiosity, diminished sleep, distractibility, and lack of judgment.[78] Secondary mania may be induced by specific drugs (e.g., levodopa, corticosteroids), by metabolic disturbances (e.g., hemodialysis), and by focal brain insults. Nearly all focal central nervous system lesions producing mania have been located in the right cerebral hemisphere, and most of the lesions have been in deep midline regions adjacent to the third ventricle.[79] The acute onset of mania in a patient over the age of 40 with no history of an affective disorder should raise consideration of secondary mania. Patients with right hemisphere lesions may be at increased risk for the development of mania.

Acute Confusional States

Confusional states are usually the result of an encephalopathy produced by a toxic or metabolic disturbance of brain function. In a few cases, however, confusional states have resulted from focal brain insults. The two focal syndromes associated with confusion are bilateral temporo-occipital lesions and right middle cerebral artery infarctions.[80,81] The latter produce profound deficits in attention without significantly depressing arousal. The confusional state resolves in 1 to 3 weeks and is attributable to interruption of the dominant attentional functions of the right hemisphere.

Paranoid Hallucinatory States

Right hemisphere lesions may also give rise to paranoid hallucinatory states. The patients suffer from persecutory delusions and ideas of reference and have auditory and visual hallucinations. The psychosis has schizophrenia-like features and closely resembles idiopathic psychosis. In most cases, the lesions associated with paranoid hallucinatory states have involved the right temporoparietal region and have been produced by vascular occlusions.[82,83]

COMMENT

The functions of the right cerebral hemisphere are complex and diverse and can be regarded as *non-dominant* or *minor* only with regard to the linguistic abilities of the left hemisphere. For many skills the right hemisphere has superior abilities. No single characteristic appears to summarize adequately the function of the right hemisphere or account for the variety of deficits that follow right hemisphere insults. Spatial and affective functions dominate the activities of the right hemisphere: in the spatial realm the right hemisphere mediates visuoperceptual function, visuomotor activities, and visuospatial memory; in the realm of affective function its integrity is necessary for the production and perception of emotional facial expression and emotional sound inflection. Flor-Henry[84] has suggested that these spatial and affective functions may share a common evolutionary history, with the visuospatial abilities concerned with territorial surveillance and the affective displays involved in territorial protection. These functions may have originally occupied both hemispheres but became lateralized to the right by the asymmetrical acquisition of language abilities by the left hemisphere.

Whatever the evolutionary background of the right hemisphere function, damage to this cerebral member gives rise to complex neurobehavioral syndromes that may include disturbances of perception, constructions, dressing, and memory as well as neuropsychiatric syndromes such as hallucinations, the Capgras delusion, and mania.

REFERENCES

1. Geschwind N, and Levitsky W: Human brain: Left-right asymmetries in temporal speech region. *Science* 1968;161:186–187.

2. Galaburda AM, LeMay M, Kemper TL, et al: Right-left asymmetries in the brain. *Science* 1978;199:852–856.

3. LeMay M, Culebras A: Human brain—morphologic differences in the hemispheres demonstrable by carotid arteriography. *N Engl J Med* 1972;287:168–170.

4. Rubens AB, Mahowald MW, Hutton JT: Asymmetry of the lateral (sylvian) fissures in man. *Neurology* 1976;26:620–624.

5. LeMay M: Morphological cerebral asymmetries of modern man, fossil man, and non-human primate. *Ann NY Acad Sci* 1976;280:349–366.

6. Falzi G, Perrone P, Vignolo LA: Right-left asymmetry in anterior speech regions. *Arch Neurol* 1982;39:239–240.

7. LeMay M: Asymmetries of the skull and handedness. *J Neurol Sci* 1977;32:243–253.

8. Pieniadz JM, Naeser MA: Computed tomographic scan cerebral asymmetries and morphologic brain asymmetries. *Arch Neurol* 1984;41:403–409.

9. Weinberger DR, Luchins DJ, Morisha J, Wyatt RJ: Asymmetrical volumes of the right and left frontal and occipital regions of the human brain. *Ann Neurol* 1982;11:97–100.

10. Kertesz A, Geschwind N: Patterns of pyramidal decussation and their relationship to handedness. *Arch Neurol* 1971;24:326–332.

11. Chi Je G, Dooling EC, Gilles FH: Left-right asymmetries of the temporal speech areas of the human fetus. *Arch Neurol* 1979;34:346–348.

12. Wada JA, Clarke R, Hamm A: Cerebral hemispheric asymmetry in humans. *Arch Neurol* 1975;32:239–246.

13. Witelson SF, Pallie W: Left hemisphere specialization for language in the newborn. *Brain* 1973;96:641–646.

14. LeMay M, Geschwind N: Hemispheric differences in the brains of great apes. *Brain Behav Evol* 1975;11:48–52.

15. Yeni-Komshian GH, Benson DA: Anatomical study of cerebral asymmetry in the temporal lobe of humans, chimpanzees, and rhesus monkeys. *Science* 1976;192:387–389.

16. Eidelberg D, Galaburda AM: Symmetry and asymmetry in the human posterior thalamus. *Arch Neurol* 1982;39:325–332.

17. Amaducci L, Sorbi S, Albanese A, et al: Choline acetyltransferase (CHAT) activity differs in right and left human temporal lobes. *Neurology* 1981;31:799–805.

18. Oke A, Keller R, Mefford I, et al: Lateralization of norepinephrine in human thalamus. *Science* 1978;200:1411–1413.

19. Starr MS, Kilpatrick IC: Bilateral asymmetry in brain GABA function? *Neurosci Lett* 1981;25:167–172.

20. Heilman KM: Neglect and related disorders, in Heilman KM, Valenstein E (eds): *Clinical Neuropsychology*. New York, Oxford University Press, 1979, pp 268–307.

21. Mesulam MM: A cortical network for directed attention and unilateral neglect. *Ann Neurol* 1981;10:309–325.

22. Watson RT, Heilman KM: Thalamic neglect. *Neurology* 1979;29:690–694.

23. Albert ML: A simple test of visual neglect. *Neurology* 1973;23:658–664.

24. Henderson VW, Alexander MP, Naeser MA: Right thalamic injury, impaired visuospatial perception, and alexia. *Neurology* 1982;32:235–240.

25. Brain WR: Visual disorientation with special reference to lesions of the right cerebral hemisphere. *Brain* 1941;64:244–272.

26. Colombo A, DeRenzi E, Gentilini M: The time course of visual hemi-inattention. *Arch Psychiatr Nervenkr* 1982;231:539–546.

27. Willanger R, Danielsen UT, Ankerhus J: Visual neglect in right-sided apoplectic lesions. *Acta Neurol Scand* 1981;64:327–336.

28. Weinstein EA, Kahn RL: The syndrome of anosognosia. *Arch Neurol Psychiatry* 1950;64:772–791.

29. Cutting J: Study of anosognosia. *J Neurol Neurosurg Psychiatry* 1978;41:548–555.

30. Weinstein EA, Kahn RL, Malitz S, et al: Delusional reduplication of parts of the body. *Brain* 1954;77:45–60.

31. Damasio A, Yamada T, Damasio H, et al: Central achromatopsia: Behavioral, anatomic, and physiologic aspects. *Neurology* 1980;30:1064–1071.

32. Green GJ, Lessell S: Acquired cerebral dyschromatopsia. *Arch Ophthalmol* 1977;95:121–128.

33. Meadows JC: Disturbed perception of colours associated with localized cerebral lesions. *Brain* 1974;97:615–632.

34. McFie J, Piercy MF, Zangwill OL: Visual-spatial agnosia associated with lesions of the right cerebral hemisphere. *Brain* 1950;73:167–190.

35. Paterson A, Zangwill OL: A case of topographical disorientation associated with a unilateral cerebral lesion. *Brain* 1945; 68:188–212.

36. Hécaen H, Tzortzis C, Rondot P: Loss of topographic memory with learning deficits. *Cortex* 1980;16:525–542.

37. Whiteley AM, Warrington EK: Selective impairment of topographical memory: A single case study. *J Neurol Neurosurg Psychiatry* 1978;41:575–578.

38. Cogan D: Visuospatial dysgnosia. *Am J Ophthalmol* 1979; 88:361–368.

39. DeRenzi E, Scotti G, Spinnler H: Perceptual and associative disorders in visual recognition. *Neurology* 1969;19:634–642.

40. Warrington EK, James M: An experimental investigation of facial recognition in patients with unilateral cerebral lesions. *Cortex* 1967;3:317–326.

41. Van Lancker DR, Canter GJ: Impairment of voice and face recognition in patients with hemispheric damage. *Brain Cognit* 1982;1:185–195.

42. Gazzaniga MS, Smylie CS: Facial recognition and brain asymmetries: Clues to underlying mechanisms. *Ann Neurol* 1983; 13:536–540.

43. Malone DR, Morris HH, Kay MC, et al: Prosopagnosia: A double dissociation between the recognition of familiar and unfamiliar faces. *J Neurol Neurosurg Psychiatry* 1982;45:820–822.

44. Cohn R, Neumann MA, Wood DH: Prosopagnosia: A clinicopathological study. *Ann Neurol* 1977;1:177–182.

45. Meadows JC: The anatomical basis of prosopagnosia. *J Neurol Neurosurg Psychiatry* 1974;37:489–501.

46. Hécaen H, Angelergues R: Agnosia for faces (prosopagnosia). *Arch Neurol* 1962;7:92–100.

47. Whiteley AM, Warrington EK: Prosopagnosia: A clinical, psychological, and anatomical study of three patients. *J Neurol Neurosurg Psychiatry* 1977;40:395–403.

48. Geschwind N: The apraxias: Neural mechanisms of disorders of learned movement. *Am Sci* 1975;63:188–195.

49. Arena R, Gianotti G: Constructional apraxia and visuopercep-

tive disabilities in relation to laterality of cerebral lesions. *Cortex* 1978;14:463–473.

50. Benson DF, Barton MI: Disturbances in constructional ability. *Cortex* 1970;6:19–46.

51. Piercy M, Hécaen H, DeAjuriaguerra J: Constructional apraxia associated with unilateral cerebral lesions—left and right sided cases compared. *Brain* 1960;83:225–242.

52. Arrigoni G, DeRenzi E: Constructional apraxia and hemispheric locus of lesion. *Cortex* 1964;1:170–197.

53. Gianotti G, Tiacci C: Patterns of drawing disability in right and left hemispheric patients. *Neuropsychologia* 1970;8:379–384.

54. Warrington EK, James M, Kinsbourne M: Drawing disability in relation to laterality of cerebral lesion. *Brain* 1966; 89:53–82.

55. Hemphill RE, Klein R: Contribution to the dressing disability as a focal sign and to the imperception phenomena. *J Ment Sci* 1948;94:611–622.

56. Ross ED: The aprosodias. *Arch Neurol* 1981;38:561–569.

57. Ross ED, Mesulam MM: Dominant language functions of the right hemisphere? *Arch Neurol* 1979;36:144–148.

58. Weintraub S, Mesulam MM, Kramer L: Disturbances in prosody. *Arch Neurol* 1981;38:742–744.

59. Heilman KM, Scholes R, Watson RT: Auditory affective agnosia. *J Neurol Neurosurg Psychiatry* 1975;38:69–72.

60. Tucker DM, Watson RT, Heilman KM: Discrimination and evocation of affectively intoned speech in patients with right parietal disease. *Neurology* 1977;27:947–950.

61. DeKosky ST, Heilman KM, Bowers D, et al: Recognition and discrimination of emotional faces and pictures. *Brain Lang* 1980;9:206–214.

62. Sackeim HA, Gur RC, Saucy MC: Emotions are expressed more intensely on the left side of the face. *Science* 1978; 202:434–436.

63. Milner B: Visual recognition and recall after right temporal-lobe excision in man. *Neuropsychologia* 1968;6:191–209.

64. Milner B: Psychological defects produced by temporal lobe excision. *Res Publ Assocn Res Nerv Ment Dis* 1958;36: 244–257.

65. Speedie LJ, Heilman KM: Anterograde memory deficits for visuospatial material after infarction of the right thalamus. *Arch Neurol* 1983;40:183–186.

66. Benson DF, Gardner H, Meadows JC: Reduplicative paramnesia. *Neurology* 1976;26:147–151.

67. Fisher CM: Disorientation for place. *Arch Neurol* 1982; 39:33–36.

68. Ruff RL, Volpe BT: Environmental reduplication associated with right frontal and parietal lobe injury. *J Neurol Neurosurg Psychiatry* 1981;44:382–386.

69. Lessell S: Higher disorders of visual function: Positive phenomena, in Glaser JS, Smith JL (eds): *Neuro-ophthalmology*. St. Louis, CV Mosby, 1975, vol VIII, pp 27–44.

70. Brust JCM, Behrens MM: "Release hallucinations" as the major symptom of posterior cerebral artery occlusion: A report of 2 cases. *Ann Neurol* 1977;2:432–436.

71. Lance JW: Simple formed hallucinations confined to the area of a specific visual field defect. *Brain* 1976;99:719–734.

72. Bender MB, Feldman M, Sobin AJ: Palinopsia. *Brain* 1968; 91:321–338.

73. Cummings JL, Syndulko K, Goldberg Z, et al: Palinopsia reconsidered. *Neurology* 1982;32:444–447.

74. Michel EM, Troost BT: Palinopsia: Cerebral localization with computed tomography. *Neurology* 1980;30:887–889.

75. Alexander MP, Stuss DT, Benson DF: Capgras' syndrome: A reduplicative phenomenon. *Neurology* 1979;29:334–339.

76. Cummings JL: Organic delusions: Phenomenology, anatomic correlations, and review. *Br J Psychiatry,* in press.

77. Hayman MA, Abrams R: Capgras' syndrome and cerebral dysfunction. *Br J Psychiatry* 1977;130:68–71.

78. Krauthammer C, Klerman GL: Secondary mania. *Arch Gen Psychiatry* 1978;35:1333–1339.

79. Cummings JL, Mendez MF: Secondary mania with focal cerebrovascular lesions. *Am J Psychiatry*, in press.

80. Medina JL, Chokroverty S, Rubino FA: Syndrome of agitated delirium and visual impairment: A manifestation of medial temporo-occipital infarction. *J Neurol Neurosurg Psychiatry* 1977;40:861–864.

81. Mesulam MM, Waxman SG, Geschwind N, Sabin TD: Acute confusional states with right middle cerebral artery infarctions. *J Neurol Neurosurg Psychiatry* 1976;39:84–89.

82. Levine DN, Finklestein S: Delayed psychosis after right temporoparietal stroke or trauma: Relation to epilepsy. *Neurology* 1982;32:267–273.

83. Peroutka SJ, Sohmer BH, Kumar AJ, et al: Hallucinations and delusions following a right temporo-parieto-occipital infarction. *Johns Hopkins Med J* 1982;151:181–185.

84. Flor-Henry P: *Cerebral Basis of Psychopathology*. Boston, John Wright-PSG Inc, 1983.

Language without Communication: The Pragmatics of Right Hemisphere Damage

Martha S. Burns, Ph.D.

Exchange #1

Clinician: Can you tell me how you got here?

J. K.: You won't believe it, but I took Amtrak from Las Vegas or rather from Kingston, Arizona, to Grand, Grand Union Station here in Vegas in Chicago.

Exchange #2

Clinician: Could you tell me what happened to you when you came to the hospital?

R. H.: Well, I hear it more from others than I recollect it. Um, but two days beforehand we were out at the club. I was enjoying myself, maybe too much but I was enjoying myself. And suddenly I . . . my words began to slur and (my thoughts always slur but my words don't) and some man, Bill Williams, Dr. Bill Williams, he's on the staff isn't he? He sent word to my waitress that he would go down in the locker room and I oughta come down and have him check him out. So you can see what improvement there's been.

Exchange #3

Clinician: Why did you have to come to the hospital?

H. P.: Well, I don't know. They say I fell and like that . . . so they didn't know what to do so the yard man, he asked the lady across the street what he should do, and she said well call the ambulance, but they wouldn't send no ambulance so they sent this . . . like a haywagon picked me up and brought me here.

All of these verbal exchanges have three things in common: (1) The basic linguistic elements—phonology, syntax, and lexical choices—are intact. (2) They are not adequate responses to the question asked. (3) They are all utterances made by patients with right cerebral damage approximately 1 month post stroke. There are, at the same time, some very striking differences among the responses; on even cursory examination each utterance seems to fail to communicate for different reasons. J. K. interprets the clinician's question literally and attempts to answer how he was transported to his present location; however, he seems to have confused cities and train stations along the way. R. H. appears to have interpreted the intent of the question appropriately but in trying to answer becomes tangential about details of the evening and is unable to tie his story together or get back to the main topic. H. P. also seems to interpret the intent of the question but expresses a lack of understanding about why she is in the hospital and a misperception of her mode of transport.

The goal of this unit is to review the current literature relevant to communication and right hemispheric cognitive potential to provide an explanation for the breakdown in the effectiveness of communication witnessed in the introductory exchanges. In the first section current psycholinguistic literature about linguistic skills will be reviewed, including phonology, syntax, and semantics, which are necessary for effective communication. Pertinent research on the role of the intact right hemisphere in cognitive processing is summarized in the second section with specific attention being directed toward cognitive functions that impact on or involve communication. Finally, the unit will conclude with a description of behavioral manifestations of right hemisphere damage that affect the communication skills of this population. By the end of this unit the introductory discourses should impart a great deal of information about the underlying disturbances of each patient.

COMMUNICATIVE COMPETENCE

Imagine for the moment a political rally. On the podium is a man whose portrait adorns banners all over the room. Buttons on lapels project his name in large red letters, and there is an air of excitement conveyed by a buzz among the participants. Suddenly the din quiets, the man moves toward the microphone, and all eyes are fixed on him in anticipation of great ideas. He opens his mouth and out comes a thin, soft, high-pitched voice. Words seem to run together without pauses; intonation is flat and monotonous. With the exception of his jaw, his face does not move. He stares down at his text without raising his eyes to the crowd. His posture is stiff, and his arms held fixed to his sides. His sentences begin to ramble on, without a point. He uses metaphors incorrectly. He cites unending details about the economy without summarizing statements or conclusions. He cannot remember punch lines of jokes, and his other attempts at humor are either not funny or inappropriate. If his intention is to inspire his audience to vote for him, his speech will probably not have the desired effect. His problem is *pragmatics*. If one dissects the speech for linguistic content, it will likely have been well articulated and grammatical and contain appropriate word choices. What is missing are the nonverbal gestures, melody, changes in loudness, facial expression, and eye contact that keep the listener interested, for example, by emphasizing main points, drawing attention to new information, and clarifying linguistic ambiguities. Furthermore, language may make sense when individual words and sentences are

interpreted separately, but the text apparently lacks cohesion, main topics are unclear, there is no humor, and attempts to make the language more interesting through colorful abstractions are in error. The listener will have difficulty maintaining attention to the speaker, perceiving his ideas, remembering important details of this talk, or following his train of thought. Pragmatics of communication is the vehicle that facilitates all of these communicative functions.

Pragmatics is broadly defined as communication in context. It encompasses the ways in which an individual uses knowledge about the situation, participants, topic at hand, previous parts of the conversation, and social conventions to make a point. Pragmatics is concerned not only with how context is used to convey information (*the proposition*) but also with how the speaker manipulates nonverbal and verbal aspects of the message to express a desired intention (*the performative*). A speaker's intention might be to persuade, like our politician; request information, like a student; or insult, like a political opponent. In this respect, the words a person chooses might have less of an impact on how the utterance is interpreted than tone of voice, inflectional contour, facial expression, and other nonverbal cues. Effective communication is that in which the content is clear (either through words or from context) and the intention behind the utterance results in its desired effect. In other words, linguistic elements must be finely integrated with nonverbal and contextual cues.[1-5]

Nonverbal Behavior Acts

One means of conveying the intent of an utterance and augmenting meaning is to vary the physical dimensions of body posture, position, gestures, facial expression, and eye contact. Often referred to as body language, these co-verbal behaviors, or communication vehicle movements, can carry meaning alone, as in a pantomime, or interface with linguistic elements of a message to clarify information or intent. Some of these physical changes are governed by social conventions, for example, how close a male and female speaker can stand when speaking casually versus intimately (*proxemics*) or how close a lecturer may stand to the front row. Deliberate violations of social conventions can be used to convey certain intentions. For example, a lecturer who wants to regain the attention of a daydreaming student might deliberately violate formal distance rules and stand directly in front of the student's chair;

similarly, a woman who is not interested in intimacy with a man may move away, as the man moves closer, to signal her lack of interest.

There are several other types of nonverbal behaviors that have communicative value. Gestural cues are often used in combination with facial expression, head nods, and eye movements to signal meaning or regulate conversational exchanges.[6] Various attempts have been made to classify these actions according to the effect they have on communication. Ekman and Friesen,[7] for example, have delineated four types of nonverbal behaviors that accompany discourse. *Adaptors* are similar to proxemic cues but are nonintentional and not governed by social convention; rather, they represent "fidgeting" types of movements such as manipulating objects, scratching, leg kicking, and so on. More intentional, but still implicit, are *regulators,* such as turn-taking signals made through shifts in eye contact or head nods, which signal a speaker about the listener's interest and desire to hear more. *Illustrators* are movements that emphasize important information or augment verbal descriptions of spatial relationships or bodily actions. Finally, *emblems* are highly structured facial expressions and/or gestures that have direct semantic value, such as the American "thumbs up" symbol meaning "good job." Similar to emblems are *pantomimes,*[4] which refer to objects, actions, and physical attributes and can be used to depict complex events. Unlike emblems, pantomimes do not usually occur naturally during conversation.[6] *Pointing* is also a nonverbal action that aids in clarifying *reference.* Nonverbal behavioral acts can thus serve a number of communicative functions; they can augment speech, substitute for speech, conflict with the verbal message signaling implicit intent, or be redundant.[4]

Other paralinguistic cues that aid communication are provided through context. Extralinguistic context includes the situation, physical setting, and type of speaking activity (e.g., sermon, speech, social exchange). The speaker and listener also provide contextual cues. Their shared knowledge about each other and the topic at hand permits *ellipsis* (deletion) of commonly known information. Our politician, for example, could have assumed from his audience that they all belong to the same political party, thereby allowing him to omit reference to his party and its philosophy. Omission of shared knowledge among participants is governed by rules of *presupposition,* which enhance communication by inclusion or deletion of specific referents. A speaker's *intention* also provides

contextual information to the listener, especially if it is explicit. For example, an angry looking parent, combined with shared knowledge that the child forgot to pick up toys, might be enough to signal to the child that he had better clean up his room. Effective communication uses these extralinguistic sources of information to perform the functions or goals that underlie a conversation.[3]

Language itself also provides contextual information that facilitates communication. Words are chosen carefully to refer to objects, actions, and events in appropriate ways. But in addition to content word choices, *reference* is also made through such conventions of dialogue as *deixis,* the ability to adjust reference from the speaker to the listener as roles in a conversation change. For example, "me" and "you" are deictic personal pronouns, "here" and "there" are deictic locatives, and "this" and "that" are deictic indefinite pronouns. There are rules that govern the use of some referential devices like pronouns. *Anaphoric* reference covers the means one may use to refer back in a dialogue (e.g., "John is nice. I like him"). *Cataphoric reference* permits referring to linguistic reference that is upcoming (e.g., "I will cover three main points").[3]

Other types of linguistic contextual cues are provided through textual devices that permit organization and aid comprehension of narrative and discourse. *Cohesion devices,* for example, permit a flow of sentences and paragraphs or utterances so that one idea logically follows from another. Other textual conventions include organizing a narrative to convey the appropriate *message sense;*[8] making complex lexical choices or metaphorical lexical combinations that aid the listener (or reader) to *derive images and motives;*[8] and *drawing conclusions, appreciating humor,* or *deriving morals.* All of these complex linguistic behaviors use linguistic context beyond the sentence level to effectively convey meaning and perform communicative functions.[5,8]

Returning to our inept politician, one can now quantify his communication breakdowns in terms of pragmatic deficiencies. He had difficulty using nonverbal behavior to help his audience attend to his propositions; he apparently had trouble using presupposition and shared knowledge to guide in his choice of information to relate; linguistic context was not used to organize his ideas by topic or help the listener comprehend new information; and his text lacked the complex linguistic features of metaphors or humor that might have created positive images or have helped the listeners to draw intended conclusions. Although the politician might have made an excellent executive, he could not communicate his skills to a group despite apparent facility with the basic structural elements of language. In this way he is quite similar to the patient with right hemisphere damage.

NEUROLOGICAL LATERALIZATION OF COGNITIVE AND COMMUNICATIVE SKILLS

The role of the right versus left hemisphere in communicative processing is far from being fully understood. While the linguists have been probing more deeply into the complexities of communicative interaction, specialists in psychology, neurology, and speech/language pathology have been applying new linguistic theories to understand more clearly how communication is processed in the normal brain (through lateralization research) and in the damaged brain (through controlled behavioral studies). The result has been an explosion of information and theory about neurological function, which may be supported or refuted as researchers refine their tools. Evidence is mounting to support the contention that basic language functions—phonology, syntax, and low-level semantics—are mediated primarily by the left hemisphere. The right hemisphere, on the other hand, is a major contributor to nonverbal, emotional aspects of communication[9] and complex aspects of linguistic processing.[4,5]

In this section pertinent information on the differential roles of the right versus left hemisphere in communicative processing will be summarized. Data are presented on the lateralization of nonverbal behavioral aspects of communication and complex linguistic skills (e.g., use of paralinguistic context, textual organization, and comprehension and understanding of abstract, metaphorical, and humorous language). Finally, data are presented from research with brain-damaged individuals that is concerned with processing limitations such as attention, orientation, and memory. Although these cognitive processes are not components of communication they affect the individual's ability to communicate.

Nonverbal Communicative Behavior

Auditory Modality

The first attempts to lateralize verbal and nonverbal communicative behaviors were made through dichotic listening studies. In the 1960s, Kimura[10,11] used dichotic presentation of competing stimuli to determine right versus left hemispheric preferences for processing different kinds of stimuli. Her initial studies revealed that whereas the right ear (left hemisphere) will show a statistical advantage discriminating between pairs of words (a different word presented to each ear), the left ear (right hemisphere) is better at discriminating melody. A logical extension of Kimura's original findings was to determine the hemispheric lateralization of intonational contour and other auditory communicative functions like nonverbal vocalizations. The results generally showed that intonational contour of speech is lateralized to the right hemisphere,[12] as are emotional tone of speech[13] and nonverbal emotional vocalization.[14,15]

Methodological changes in dichotic presentations have revealed that one can change lateralization preferences by altering some facets of a stimulus over others. For example, Bryden and Ley[16] have shown that *priming*, rehearsing or thinking about, verbal material activates the left hemisphere to process information that the right hemisphere might normally process while *priming* with spatial images activates the right hemisphere. Using dichotically presented word lists and visual (tachistoscopic) presentations of cartoon faces (right hemispheric preference), these investigators were able to shift lateralization by priming subjects with high imagery and affective word lists. Results confirmed that the right hemisphere has a special role in processing emotional and high imagery stimuli, even if they are words. Subject variables also play a part in lateralization. For example, skilled musicians and Morse code users show right ear effects (left hemisphere) for music[17] and Morse code[18] while novices show right hemispheric processing of these stimuli.

Studies of adults with right hemisphere damage have revealed disturbances in expression and comprehension of speech prosody,[19,20] inability to produce intoned sentences on command or comprehend emotional tone of speech,[21] as well as disturbances in recognition of familiar voices.[22]

Visual Modality

Visual lateralization studies have used models largely adapted from the dichotic literature. In general, they have shown right visual field advantages (presumed left hemispheric specialization) for verbal material when tasks require language processing. Some of the major limitations of the visual research studies stem from the reliance on verbal response paradigms that may bias processing to the left hemisphere and the natural tendency for readers of English to scan a page from left to right during reading. (See Bryden[23] for a review of the studies and limitations to the designs.) To counter some of these problems, researchers have made methodological changes in design, such as writing words vertically instead of horizontally, but because of methodological differences from study to study results have been quite varied.

Original lateralization studies showed a right hemispheric preference for nonverbal visual and visuospatial tasks, including depth perception,[24] color discrimination,[25,26] and estimates of numbers in dot displays.[27] Nonverbal communication behaviors are also lateralized to the right hemisphere. For example, Ley and Bryden[28] and Strauss and Moscovitch[29] found that perception of emotion on faces showed a left visual field effect. There is some question as to the validity of these findings, however, since facial recognition in general shows a left visual field advantage. It has been difficult experimentally to tease out facial expression lateralization from facial recognition lateralization.[9,30] Expressive facial movements have also been studied in normal populations to determine whether "facedness" is lateralized. Borod and colleagues,[9] for example, found that normal left- and right-handed adults show significantly more movement on the left side of the face than on the right while making posed expressions. Moscovitch[30] also found more asymmetry of movement during spontaneous facial expression in the lower left side of the face. Unlike Borod and colleagues, however, Moscovitch did not find such an asymmetry in left-handed individuals. Moscovitch interprets this and other similar findings as supportive of mediation by the right hemisphere of voluntary control of facial expression.

Among brain-damaged populations, those with right hemisphere lesions are often described as displaying "flat affect" (see Myers[31] for an excellent review), although the research results have been mixed. Buck and Duffy[32] found that patients with right-sided lesions showed less facial expressiveness when viewing affective slides than those with left-sided lesions. However, Heilman and Valenstein[33] failed to find differences between the two populations. Prosopagnosia (impaired facial recognition) is generally associated with right hemisphere damage.[34–36] Data suggest that the disturbance improves fairly quickly compared with other disturbances, such as constructional apraxia, and that improvement is highly correlated with age, with faster recovery being evident among younger patients.[37] Strub and Black[38] believe that prosopagnosia is usually due to bilateral involvement. (See also Unit 2 for a discussion of prosopagnosia.)

Motoric and Tactile Modalities

Since most adults are right handed (left hemisphere dominant) for gross motor, fine motor, and praxis skills, variance in dominance for tactile perception has been difficult to research. It has been generally assumed that gestural skills require praxis and therefore will show left hemisphere control. (See Foldi and co-workers[4] for a discussion of the relationship between praxis and gesture in neurological research). Most of the research has indicated that patients with left hemisphere damage show disturbances in comprehension and spontaneous use of gesture. When compared with patients with right hemisphere damage and normal controls, aphasics show impaired ability to recognize pantomimes[39,40] and comprehend gestures alone or in combination with spoken messages.[6] Goodglass and Kaplan[41] found aphasics to be more impaired than those with right hemisphere damage on use of "natural" and "conventional" gestures. Cicone and colleagues[42] found that gestural impairments in aphasics generally mirror expressive speech characteristics: for anterior aphasics, gestures are concrete and sparse but clear; in posterior aphasics, gestures are abundant and fluent but vague or general. Foldi and co-workers[4] suggest that use of less symbolic gestures (such as contextually based gestures that regulate turn-taking) may not be impaired in aphasia. Lemon and associates[43] noted a generalized reduction in spontaneous use of body posture and gesture for emphasis or to signal turn-taking among patients with right hemisphere damage with apparently spared ability to gesture on command. Because these observations were based on a small clinical population (12 patients) without control groups, the findings require verification. It seems worth noting, however, that some lateralization research is showing a right-handed (left hemisphere) advantage for tasks that require sequencing patterns and a left-handed preference for tasks that required spatial processing.[44] It will be interesting to follow the research in this area to determine whether spatial tasks, emotionally inspired gestures, or gestures that occur spontaneously as part of paralinguistic discourse cues will show differential right versus left hemispheric preferences.

In summary, the right hemisphere seems to mediate processing tasks that involve emotion, visual imagery, visuospatial perception, intonation and other nonverbal vocalizations, facial recognition, and perception and production of facial expression. From the perspective of nonverbal communication behaviors, the right hemisphere appears to process auditory and visual but perhaps not gestural paralinguistic cues. Right hemisphere damage impairs use of prosody and facial expression.

Complex Linguistic Skills

Disturbances of verbal skills associated with right hemisphere lesions have been reported as early as 1962 by Jon Eisenson.[45] Other reports of language impairment in patients with unilateral right hemisphere damage followed, but the nature of the deficits remained unclear. For example, Marcie and associates, as discussed in Hier and Kaplan,[46] reported disorders of expressive language including articulation, prosody, syntax, and semantics among a group of 28 patients with right hemisphere damage. They believed that the problems might have been an artifact of other components of dysfunction such as perseveration. Other researchers reported similar findings, but they remained reluctant to attribute reduced language performance among patients with right-sided lesions to a primary linguistic disturbance. Swisher and Sarno[47] reported reduced performance on Parts IV and V of the *Token Test* among patients with right-sided brain damage but proposed that visuospatial or attentional deficits might have been a factor. Archibald and Wepman[48] reported that 8 of 22 patients with right hemisphere damage performed poorly on Wepman's *Language Modalities Test for Aphasia,* again citing such possible contributory factors as attentional deficit, dementia, or possible bilateral lesion involvement.

It was not until the 1970s that verbal deficits were examined as an actual phenomenon associated with damage to the right hemisphere. The tide began to turn after "split brain" research showed that the isolated right hemisphere has some receptive language capabilities.[49] Since that time, attempts have been made to specify more clearly the nature of right cerebral language dysfunction. Disturbances in comprehension of logical syllogisms,[50] pictorial interpretation of metaphors,[51] and concrete interpretations of proverbs[46] have suggested that abstract verbal tasks pose a particu-

lar problem for this population. It is interesting that metaphorical language and proverbs are problematical for patients with right hemisphere damage, since from a linguistic standpoint this figurative language has a semantic role akin to referential meaning of single words. In other words, to understand the meaning of a "heavy heart" or "raining cats and dogs," one must avoid analysis of the word-by-word sequence and recognize the sequence as a single meaningful entity— "sad" and "hard rain," respectively. Analysis of idioms and proverbs sequentially will result in a concrete or literal interpretation of the sequence, as has been observed by some of the researchers.[46]

In a review of these and other recent investigations on the role of the right hemisphere in processing language, Gardner and associates[5] conclude that "even the most hallowed sanctuary for the left hemisphere— that of language competence—has recently been challenged."

Foldi and co-workers[4] add that despite the right hemisphere-damaged patients' competence with literal language they are "severely disadvantaged" because of difficulties with abstract meanings, problems organizing and comprehending narratives, and difficulties interpreting jokes and metaphors. Gardner and colleagues[5] elaborate further that experiments in their own laboratory document that when compared with patients with left hemisphere damage, those with right-sided lesions exhibit problems with antonyms, excessive and rambling spontaneous speech, tendency to focus on insignificant details, use of tangential remarks, difficulties in appreciation of humor, and problems arranging sentences into a coherent narrative. The investigators explain the range of disturbances as reflecting an unawareness or insensitivity to rules that govern discourse, especially in the use of context. Such disturbances generally fall under the rubric of pragmatics of language, as discussed earlier in this unit. In addition to complex linguistic disturbances, however, these patients also demonstrate problems with other high-level cognitive tasks requiring language including syllogistic reasoning.[50]

OTHER COMMUNICATION-RELATED DISTURBANCES OF RIGHT HEMISPHERE DAMAGE

Disturbances of nonverbal visual skills have been reported throughout the literature on right hemisphere damage. The visuomotor disturbance characterized as constructional apraxia was among the earliest disturbances attributed to unilateral right hemisphere damage.[52] In 1979, Kertesz and co-workers[53] noted that of 18 patients with unilateral nondominant hemisphere lesions confirmed by computed tomography, 6 showed severe constructional apraxia as determined through use of block design and drawing tests. They reported that most of these patients also showed problems with other visuospatial tasks and left-sided neglect. Furthermore, significant reading problems were observed in 3 of the patients with constructional apraxia. Hier and associates[53] performed a factor analysis on behavior patterns exhibited by 41 patients with unilateral right hemisphere lesions and found that constructional apraxia correlated highly with unilateral spatial neglect and was associated with right parietal lesions. Kertesz and co-workers[54] did not report the parietal lesion but rather large central lesions. (See Unit 2 for a discussion of the roles of the right and left hemispheres in constructional skills.)

Problems with visuospatial perception have also been identified as a frequent manifestation of unilateral right hemisphere damage.[55] Such visuospatial tasks as determination of line slant[56] and identifying rotated stick figures[57] present difficulties for the patient with right hemisphere damage.

A final visual disturbance that has been described as associated with a unilateral right hemisphere lesion is color recognition. Both tasks of requiring color matching and color sorting have been identified as disturbed in these patients;[58,59] however, some researchers believe that bilateral lesions are necessary to produce an agnosia for colors.[60,61]

From the previous discussion, it seems apparent that visuoperceptual and visuomotor problems can be considered a hallmark of right hemisphere damage. In fact, in a study of the prevalence of various behavioral abnormalities after right-sided brain injury, Hier and associates[53] found that constructional apraxia was evident in 93% of the patients examined and that unilateral spatial neglect was evident in 85% of the patients. Not only were these disturbances the most prevalent behavioral abnormalities observed, the symptomatology persisted beyond 60 weeks post stroke for some patients. On the surface, visual perception might seem a major specialization of the right hemisphere from these data. The findings that some aspects of reading are lateralized to the right hemisphere in subjects with no brain damage and that left hemisphere lesions consistently

produce alexia suggest that visual perception is like auditory perception in that it is affected differentially depending on the task. It appears that visual tasks that require integrative perception (e.g., visuospatial perception, color recognition, and face recognition) and affective perception are those most severely affected by right hemisphere damage. The reading impairments observed in these patients have been associated with general visuoperceptual and visuomotor impairment.[54] Rather than problems with comprehension of the written word, reading impairments seem more related to problems with visual scanning, tracking from left to right (visuospatial orientation), and neglect of left hemispace.[43,62]

A last area of disturbance associated with right hemisphere damage is that of impaired ability to express emotion and denial of illness. In a major study of emotional response to stroke, Gianotti, as reported by Bryden,[23] compared the incidence of catastrophic reactions (i.e., swearing and crying) with indifference reactions (i.e., joking and denial of illness) among 150 patients with unilateral lesions. Results demonstrated that 62% of the patients with left hemisphere damage versus 10% of those with right hemisphere damage showed catastrophic reactions while the opposite pattern held for indifference reactions. Anosognosia (denial of illness) is highly associated with right hemisphere lesions.[63,64] In fact, Hécaen[65] reports that anosognosia is seven times as common among patients with right-sided lesions as compared with those with left-sided lesions. It seems likely, at least to some extent, that the right hemisphere–damaged patient's lack of catastrophic reaction to the illness may stem from the lack of awareness that the illness exists.

Anosognosia, in turn, may not reflect so much a "denial" of deficit as an imperception. Hier and associates[37] performed a factor analysis on 12 behavioral disturbances among 41 patients with right hemisphere lesions. One factor that emerged, Factor I, was described as "inattention" factor and included inability to sustain attention, inability to direct attention to the left side of space (the hemiplegic side of the body), and denial of the left hemiplegia. This same factor was also correlated with problems of facial recognition and constructional apraxia. It seems possible from these results that patients who have severe visuoperceptual problems and neglect of the left hemispace are unaware of the hemiplegia or the severe effects of the stroke.

CONCLUSION—METHODOLOGIES THAT CAN BE DERIVED

The research on lateralization in the intact brain and effects of right hemisphere damage points to several areas of function/dysfunction that seem to be largely mediated by the right hemisphere. As a general dichotomy, the data suggest that the left hemisphere is largely concerned with processing of an analytic nature. This is especially true for temporal analysis, as seen in auditory analysis of speech and language, and in spatial analysis, as is required for reading and somatosensory responses. The right hemisphere seems to process information in an integrative or gestalt fashion, especially in spatial recognition of visual stimuli. Auditory recognition of sequences as a unit also seems a right hemispheric function, as in such skills as melody and prosody perception and in comprehension of idioms. The right hemisphere also seems to play a major role in perception and expression of affect and in some cases may override the left hemisphere's verbal dominance in processing affectively or high imagery-loaded verbal material.[16]

Semmes[66] has speculated a neurophysiological model for the hemispheric processing distinction that is quite compelling. She suggests that whereas evidence to date points to the highly localized neurophysiology of the left hemisphere, right hemispheric representation is more diffusely organized. Hier and associates[53] reported findings that right hemispheric behavior manifestations of damage are more related to overall size of the lesion than locus. This being the case, Semmes speculates that the right hemisphere would be better able to integrate information across and within modalities.

With this possible explanation for hemispheric asymmetries of function in mind, a summary of the behavioral manifestations of right hemisphere damage that have been identified can be used to guide clinical diagnosis and interpretation of symptomatology. It seems useful in this regard to use an organization of symptomatology that incorporates the apparent integrative function of the right hemisphere, as opposed to the more modality-specific organization commonly associated with left hemispheric processes. Accordingly, a clinical model of processing levels adapted from the learning disabilities literature[67] provides a useful organizational framework for categorizing deficits of the right hemisphere.

Attentional Deficits

Hier and associates[53] have identified attributes of "inattention" as a primary factor of right hemisphere dysfunction. Inability to focus and maintain attention has also been described by others as a salient characteristic of this population.[68] Attentional disturbances in this population seem to include not only problems with attentional focus to a task but also inattention to left hemispace (neglect) and anosognosia (denial of illness).

Perceptual Deficits

Visuoperceptual impairment is a hallmark of the syndrome of right hemisphere dysfunction and affects reading,[54] visuospatial performance,[55–57] visuomotor performance,[53,54] and facial recognition.[34,53] Auditory perceptual skills are also affected in patients with right hemisphere damage, especially those perceptual tasks that require perception of an auditory configuration as a unit. Processing of nonverbal vocalizations[14] and prosodic inflection[19] appear to fall under right hemispheric specialization. Similarly, perception and expression of nonverbal communication signals[43] and emotional expression[23] are affected by right hemisphere lesions.

Orientation

Although not addressed specifically in the review of the literature on right hemisphere dysfunction because of the lack of specific data on the subject, the presence of orientation problems among patients with right-sided lesions is discussed by at least one author. Fisher[69] presented a case study of a patient with a right temporoparietal lesion who showed severe problems with orientation to place. Given the severity of visuospatial perception and inattention among patients with right hemisphere damage, it seems likely that disorientation to place would be a common sequela of such lesions, especially in early stages of recovery. Clinical experience suggests such disorientation is, in fact, quite common. Disorientation to time has been observed as well.[70] This seems to be related to the patients' difficulty in telling time because of visuoperceptual impairment, as well as to problems of monitoring the passage of time. Controlled investigation of orientation disturbances in the right hemisphere–damaged population is an important next step in research because of the profound clinical implications for prognostication and rehabilitation. One might also expect problems with orientation to person because of difficulties with facial recognition, although this has not been reported specifically in the literature. It may be that orientation to person is not a problem because the patients are able to use vocal cues to compensate for visual impairments, although Van Lancker and Canter[22] have indicated that recognition of familiar voices is impaired in some patients with right-sided lesions.

Memory

Memory was also not specifically addressed in the review since the literature is limited in specifying types of memory impairments that characterize right hemisphere damage. The literature is replete with references to retention disturbances stemming from damage to either hemisphere.[38,71–73] Studies of brain-damaged subjects suggest that memory for some types of nonverbal material is selectively impaired in the patient with right hemisphere damage. Riege and co-workers[74] found that when compared with patients with left hemisphere damage with aphasia and with normal adults, patients with right hemisphere damage showed greater disturbances on short-term and long-term recognition of geometric art designs and bird-call patterns. Aphasics performed more poorly on verbal recognition tasks. Similarly, Whitehouse[75] compared recognition of words and pictures in an equal number of patients with right- and left-sided lesions. The study showed that those with left hemisphere damage performed better on picture recognition and those with right hemisphere damage performed better on word recognition tasks. Of specific interest was the additional finding that when an intervening task was interpolated between presentation of an item and the recognition task, the two groups again responded differently. The aphasics' performance was most disrupted by imaginal intervening tasks, while the patients with right hemisphere damage suffered from verbal intervening tasks. Whitehouse speculates that these tasks interfered with the patients' storage strategies—verbal storage strategies for those with right-sided lesions and nonverbal storage strategies for the aphasics.

Research by Moscovitch[30] generally provides support for the suggestion that memory for visual images is lateralized in the right hemisphere; however, he has also found that verbal memory tasks that require reten-

tion of high imagery or high affective words result in a "priming" shift to right hemispheric lateralization. Wechsler's[76] research with patients with right hemisphere damage provides support for the role of the right hemisphere in retention of emotionally charged material. He found that emotionally charged stimuli were better retained by these patients than neutral stimuli.

The available data suggest that memory impairment is likely a manifestation of brain damage in general, but that left and right hemisphere lesions lead to different types of impairment. Memory disturbances seem to conform to the same differential processes evident in the perceptual and expressive domains.

Integration

Since the research in lateralization and dysfunction of the right hemisphere points to integrative functions as a specialization of right hemispheric processing, it would be expected that integration tasks such as logical reasoning and verbal abstraction would pose problems for these patients. The literature confirms this expectation, indicating that patients with right hemisphere damage experience difficulties with complex linguistic and visuospatial reasoning tasks.[4,5,46,50,51,77]

POSTSCRIPT

Returning to the verbal exchanges at the beginning of this unit, it is now possible to understand the nature of difficulties experienced by each patient. In each case the individual showed difficulty organizing narrative description and maintaining the topic. But, beyond that, J. K. seemed to demonstrate severe difficulties interpreting the implicit intention of the question (knowledge most persons would glean from the context of the interview) and had problems perceiving space and time as they related to the trip from Las Vegas to Chicago. The clinician might anticipate from this expressed confusion that the patient would show disturbances in passive or active orientation to place as well, which in fact was borne out in clinical reports.

R. H.'s discourse sample demonstrates the complex linguistic disturbances associated with organization of text. He quickly digressed from the topic and was unable to return to it. He also showed some problems with temporal and/or spatial organization of events surrounding his hospital admission. (The listener is unclear whether he was admitted the evening he was at the club or whether the club event happened 2 days before admission.) The patient also presupposed too much from the listener, jumping from the doctor checking him out to the improvement he had made. Note finally that his story is told as he ''hears'' it from others. This may be an indication of the patient's reliance on verbal knowledge to aid retention.

The final exchange, with H. P., illustrates disturbances not quite so obvious in the others' narratives. The sample suggests severe visual misperception of the ambulance (which did bring her to the hospital) and anosognosia (the patient had a severe hemiplegia and had been told repeatedly that she had a stroke).

It is important to recognize that all of these patients showed difficulty communicating because of complex linguistic impairments in addition to other attentional, perceptual, orientation, and memory problems, the sum of which rendered their narratives confused and disorganized. That physicians, psychologists, and speech/language pathologists have failed to observe these communication difficulties for so many years seems now one of the major paradoxes in clinical diagnosis of neurologically impaired adults.

REFERENCES

1. Bates E: Intentions, conventions, and symbols, in Bates E. (ed): *The Emergence of Symbols: Cognition and Communication in Infancy*. New York, Academic Press, 1980, pp 33–68.
2. Dore J: A description of early language development. *J Psycholinguist Res* 1974; 4:423–430.
3. Lund N, Duchan N: *Assessing Children's Language in Naturalistic Contexts*. Englewood Cliffs, NJ, Prentice-Hall, 1983.
4. Foldi NS, Cicone M, Gardner H: Pragmatic aspects of communication in brain-damaged patients, in Segalowitz S (ed): *Language Functions and Brain Organization*. New York, Academic Press, 1983, pp 51–86.
5. Gardner H, Brownell H, Wapner W, et al: Missing the point: The role of the right hemisphere in the processing of complex linguistic materials, in Perecman E (ed): *Cognitive Processing in the Right Hemisphere*. New York, Academic Press, 1983, pp 169–191.
6. Venus CA: *The Effect of Gestural Cues on Aphasics' Comprehension of Spoken Messages,* unpublished doctoral dissertation. Northwestern University, 1983.
7. Ekman P, Friesen W: The repertoire of non-verbal behavior: Categories, origins, usage, and coding. *Semiotica* 1969;1: 49–98.
8. Luria A: *Language and Cognition,* Wertsch J (ed). New York, John Wiley & Sons, 1981.
9. Borod JC, Koff E, Caron HS: Right hemispheric specialization for the expression and appreciation of emotion: A focus on the face, in Perecman E (ed): *Cognitive Processing in the Right Hemisphere*. New York, Academic Press, 1983, pp 83–110.
10. Kimura D: Cerebral dominance and the perception of verbal stimuli. *Can J Psychol* 1961;15:166–171.
11. Kimura D: Left-right differences in the perception of melodies. *Q J Psychol* 1964;16:355–358.
12. Blumstein S, Cooper WE: Hemispheric processing of intonational contours. *Cortex* 1972;8:146–158.
13. Haggard MP, Parkinson AM: Stimulus and task factors in the perceptual lateralization of speech signals. *Q J Exp Psychol* 1971;23:168–177.
14. King FL, Kimura D: Left-ear superiority in dichotic perception of vocal, non-verbal sounds. *Can J Psychol* 1972;26:111–116.
15. Carmon A, Nachson I: Ear asymmetry in perception of emotional non-verbal stimuli. *Acta Psychol* 1973;37:351–359.
16. Bryden MP, Ley RG: Right hemispheric involvement in imagery and affect, in Perecman E (ed): *Cognitive Processing in the Right Hemisphere*. New York, Academic Press, 1983, pp 111–124.
17. Bever TG, Chiarello RJ: Cerebral dominance in musicians and nonmusicians. *Science* 1974;185:537–539.
18. Papçun G, Krashen S, Terbeek D, et al: Is the left hemisphere specialized for speech, language and/or something else? *J Acoust Soc Am* 1974;55:319–327.
19. Ross ED, Mesulam M: Dominant language functions of the right hemisphere? *Arch Neurol* 1979;36:144–148.
20. Ross ED: The aprosodias. *Arch Neurol* 1981;38:561–569.
21. Tucker D, Watson RT, Heilman KM: Discrimination and evocation of affectively intoned speech in patients with parietal disease. *Neurology* 1977;27:947–950.
22. Van Lancker DR, Canter GJ: Impairment of voice and face recognition in patients with hemispheric damage. *Brain Cognition* 1982;1:185–195.
23. Bryden MP: *Laterality: Functional Asymmetry in the Intact Brain*. New York, Academic Press, 1982.
24. Kimura D, Durnford M: Normal studies on the function of the right hemisphere in vision, in Dimond S, Beaumont J (eds): *Hemisphere Function in the Human Brain*. New York, John Wiley & Sons, 1974.
25. Davidoff JB: Hemispheric differences in dot detection. *Cortex* 1977;13:434–444.
26. Hannay HJ: Asymmetry in reception and retention of colors. *Brain Lang* 1979;8:191–201.
27. Hilliard RD: Hemispheric laterality effects on facial recognition tasks in normal subjects. *Cortex* 1973;9:246–258.
28. Ley RG, Bryden MP: Hemispheric differences in recognizing faces and emotions. *Brain Lang* 1979;7:137–138.
29. Strauss E, Moscovitch M: Perception of facial expressions. *Brain Lang* 1981;13:308–332.

30. Moscovitch M: The linguistic and emotional functions of the normal right hemisphere, in Perecman E (ed): *Cognitive Processing in the Right Hemisphere*. New York, Academic Press, 1983, pp 57–82.

31. Myers PM: Right hemisphere impairment, in Holland A (ed): *Language Disorders in Adults*. San Diego, College-Hill Press, 1984.

32. Buck R, Duffy RJ: Non-verbal communication of affect in brain damaged patients. *Cortex* 1980;16:351–362.

33. Heilman KM, Valenstein E: *Clin Neuropsychol*. New York, Oxford University Press, 1979.

34. Hécaen H, Angelergues R: Agnosia for faces (prosopagnosia). *Arch Neurol* 1962;7:92–100.

35. Benton AL, Van Allen MW: Impairment in facial recognition in patients with cerebral disease. *Cortex* 1968;4:344–358.

36. Meadows JC: The anatomical basis of prosopagnosia. *J Neurol Neurosurg Psychiatry* 1974;37:489–501.

37. Hier DB, Mondlock J, Caplan LR: Recovery of behavioral abnormalities after right hemisphere stroke. *Neurology* 1983;33:345–350.

38. Strub RL, Black FW: *The Mental Status Examination in Neurology*. Philadelphia, FA Davis, 1977.

39. Duffy RJ, Duffy J, Pearson K: Pantomime recognition in aphasia. *J Speech Hear Res* 1975;18:115–132.

40. Gianotti G, Lemmo MA: Comprehension of symbolic gestures in aphasia. *Brain Lang* 1976;3:451–460.

41. Goodglass H, Kaplan E: Disturbances in gesture and pantomime in aphasia. *Brain* 1963;86:703–720.

42. Cicone M, Wapner W, Foldi N, Zurif E, Gardner H. The relation between gesture and language in aphasic communication. *Brain Lang* 1979;8:324–349.

43. Lemon P, Burns M, Lehner L: Communication deficits associated with right cerebral brain damage. Presented at the American Speech-Language-Hearing Association Convention, Atlanta, 1979.

44. Nachson I, Carmon A: Hand preference in sequential and spatial discrimination tasks. *Cortex* 1975;11:123–131.

45. Eisenson J: Language and intellectual modifications associated with right cerebral damage. *Lang Speech* 1962;5:49–53.

46. Hier DB, Kaplan J: Verbal comprehension deficits after right hemisphere damage. *Appl Psycholinguist* 1980;1:279–294.

47. Swisher LP, Sarno MT: Token test scores of three matched patient groups: Left brain damaged with aphasia, right brain damaged without aphasia, non-brain-damaged. *Cortex* 1969; 5:264–273.

48. Archibald TM, Wepman JM: Language disturbances and non-verbal cognitive performance in eight patients following injury to the right hemisphere. *Brain* 1968;91:117–130.

49. Zaidel E: Auditory vocabulary of the right hemisphere following brain bisection or hemidecortication. *Cortex* 1976; 12:191–211.

50. Caramazza A, Gordon J, Zurif EB, et al: Right-hemispheric damage and verbal problem solving behavior. *Brain Lang* 1976;3:41–46.

51. Winner E, Gardner H: The comprehension of metaphor in brain damaged patients. *Brain* 1977;100:717–729.

52. Piercy MF, Hécaen H, Ajuriaguerra J: Constructional apraxia associated with unilateral cerebral lesions. *Brain* 1960;83: 225–242.

53. Hier DB, Mondlock J, Caplan LR: Behavioral abnormalities after right hemisphere stroke. *Neurology* 1983;33:337–344.

54. Kertesz A, Harlock W, Coates R: Computer tomographic localization, lesion size, and prognosis in aphasia and non-verbal impairment. *Brain Lang* 1979;8:34–50.

55. Benton AL: Disorders of spatial orientation, in Vinken P, Bruyn G (eds): *Handbook of Clinical Neurology: Disorders of Higher Nervous Activity*. Amsterdam, North-Holland, 1969, vol 3, pp 312–328.

56. Benton AL, Hannay HJ, Varney NR: Visual perception of line direction in patients with unilateral brain disease. *Neurology* 1975;25:907–910.

57. Berlucci G, Brizzolara D, Marzi CA, et al: The role of the stimulus discriminability and verbal codability in hemispheric specialization for visuospatial tasks. *Neuropsychologia* 1979;17:195–202.

58. DeRenzi E, Spinnler H: Impaired performance on color tasks in patients with hemispheric damage. *Cortex* 1967;3:194–217.

59. Scotti G, Spinnler H: Colour imperception in unilateral hemisphere damaged patients. *J Neurol Neurosurg Psychiatry* 1970;33:22–28.

60. Geschwind N: Disconnexion syndromes in animals and man. *Brain* 1965;88:237–294, 585–644.

61. Meadows JC: Disturbed perception of colors associated with localized cerebral lesions. *Brain* 1974;97:615–632.

62. Diller L, Gordon WA, Gerstmann LJ, et al: Training sensory awareness and spatial organization in people with right brain damage. *Arch Phys Med Rehabil* 1979;60:491–496.

63. Critchley M: *The Parietal Lobes*. London, Arnold, 1953.

64. Flor-Henry P: Lateralized temporal-limbic dysfunction and psychopathology. *Ann NY Acad Sci* 1976;280:777–795.

65. Hécaen H: Clinical symptomatology in right and left hemispheric lesions, in Mountcastle VB (ed): *Interhemispheric Relations and Cerebral Dominance*. Baltimore, Johns Hopkins Press, 1962, pp 215–243.

66. Semmes J: Hemispheric specialization: A possible clue to mechanism. *Neuropsychologia* 1968;6:11–26.

67. Johnson D, Mykelbust H: *Learning Disabilities: Educational Principles and Practices*. New York, Grune & Stratton, 1967.

68. Dimond S: *The Double Brain*. Baltimore, Williams & Wilkins, 1972.

69. Fisher CM: Disorientation for place. *Arch Neurol* 1982;39: 33–36.

70. Burns MS, Halper AS, Mogil SM: *Communication Problems in Right Hemispheric Brain Damage*. Chicago, Rehabilitation Institute of Chicago, 1983.

71. Strub RL, Black FW: *Organic Brain Syndromes: An Introduction to Neurobehavioral Disorders*. Philadelphia, FA Davis, 1981.

72. Hécaen H, Albert ML: *Human Neuropsychology*. New York, John Wiley & Sons, 1978.

73. Wilson BA, Moffet N: *Clinical Management of Memory Problems*. Rockville, MD, Aspen Systems Corporation, 1984.

74. Riege WH, Metter EJ, Hanson WR: Verbal and non-verbal recognition memory in aphasic and nonaphasic stroke patients. *Brain Lang* 1980;10:60–70.

75. Whitehouse PJ: Imagery and verbal encoding in left and right hemisphere damaged patients. *Brain Lang* 1981;14:315–332.

76. Wechsler AF: The effect of organic brain disease on recall of emotionally charged versus neutral narrative tests. *Neurology* 1973;23:130–135.

77. Wapner W, Hambry S, Gardner H: The role of the right hemisphere in the apprehension of complex linguistic materials. *Brain Lang* 1981;14:15–33.

Diagnosis of Communication Problems in Right Hemisphere Damage

Martha S. Burns, Ph.D., CCC-SP, Anita S. Halper, M.A., CCC-SP, and Shelley I. Mogil, M.S., CCC-SP

The first three units of this book highlighted the explosion of research and information erupting from within the many psychoneurological disciplines interested in the function of the right hemisphere. The practical and theoretical value of this information is unquestionable. As each new nuance of processing is clarified or a new symptom of a lesion recognized, clinical scientists broaden their understanding of cognitive processing and of the remarkable biological machine that makes such processing possible—the human brain. From this research base it is the job of the clinician to apply the data accumulated to develop practical and objective diagnostic tools. The best tools should efficiently tap not only those processes uniquely vulnerable to the right hemisphere lesion but also those impairments likely to have the greatest vocational and avocational significance. It is with these objectives in mind that the tests and rating scales presented in this chapter were developed and that certain standardized tests are recommended as a protocol for evaluation of right hemisphere dysfunction.

Prior to presentation of the recommended diagnostic protocol it is important to review the research generalizations on which the development of the protocol was founded.

Unlike the modality specific deficits associated with left hemisphere lesions, right hemisphere lesions seem to interfere with more general processing capacities, such as attention and perception[1] and organization and integration.[2]

Although there seem to be general patterns of right versus left cerebral organization, there are also individual differences. It is generally accepted that brain structure and hemisphere function differ according to sex and handedness. However, research now also points to differences in cerebral organization resulting from varying developmental experiences and/or different cognitive style. Such individual differences make each person unique in his neurological premorbid processing capabilities.[3] It is therefore just as important for the clinician to use tests that are designed to demonstrate processing strengths and intact capabilities as it is to catalogue lesion-related limitations. Although the latter provide objective indexes of impairment, it is the former that the clinician must capitalize on in developing compensatory therapeutic strategies.

Whereas left hemisphere damage is associated with specific disorders in analysis of stimuli, most notably literal analysis of language, right-sided damage is more likely to affect gestalt perception and complex aspects of language. Language disturbances include interpretation of metaphorical language and use of linguistic and nonlinguistic context.[2,4]

As a summary, processing capabilities that are likely to be affected by right hemisphere damage include the following:

- attention—especially problems with focusing attention, impulsivity, left-sided neglect, and anosognosia.[1,5]

- orientation—especially problems in orientation to time and place because of perceptual deficits that appear to interfere with the use of visual and temporal cues within the environment.[6,7]
- perception—these disturbances are a hallmark of this syndrome, especially visual perception of space, facial recognition, perception of emotional affect, and perceptual skills required for reading, writing, and calculation. Auditory perceptual disturbances are also observed, including problems with perception of environmental sounds, melodies and chords, and speech prosody.[1,8]
- pragmatic communication disorders—including disorders in use and interpretation of affective language,[4,5,9] use and interpretation of contextual cues,[2,5,8] and use and interpretation of paralinguistic cues, including intonation and facial expression.[9-11]
- memory disturbances—especially affecting retention of visually coded material and visual imagery skills.[12-14]
- integration disturbances—including problems with verbal problem solving,[15] interpretation of metaphorical language,[16] appreciation of humor,[5,17] and disturbances in organization and comprehension of discourse and narratives.[2,5]

The diagnostic battery presented in this unit has been developed from the previously summarized research base. Tests and rating scales have been specifically designed to focus on those known sequelae of right hemisphere damage that have implications to the rehabilitative process. When possible, numerical values and/or objective indexes of behavioral limitations are used. Values have been assigned according to the degree to which the patient deviates from a general standard of "adequacy" rather than "normalcy." The standard of "adequacy" was chosen to permit the clinician to consider individual differences in cognitive style and evaluate each person relative to his premorbid processing characteristics rather than comparing performance to a statistical norm. This is especially important when evaluating such behaviors as communicative competence since communication style is known to vary across socioeconomic class as well as by sex and age. However, because of the subjective nature of rating scales, the recommended diagnostic battery also includes commercially available standardized assessment tools. The majority of the available standardized

tests were not developed specifically for the population with right-sided brain damage; nonetheless, they are applicable for brain-damaged populations in general and do provide norms for objectifying the severity of impairment relative to other adult populations and/or for determining the value of treatment.

OBJECTIVES OF THE EVALUATION

As in the examination of any neurologically impaired patient, evaluation of the patient with right hemisphere damage will be guided by diagnostic, prognostic, and therapeutic objectives. First, evaluation must establish pretreatment baseline measures for later measurement of recovery. For this purpose, standardized tests of language performance and academic skills provide data on specific abilities for comparison with normal populations. Although premorbid levels must always be considered, normative data provide estimates of severity of disorder, assist other professionals, and provide quantitative measures for posttreatment comparison.

A second major goal of evaluation of this population is to assist in developing prognostic predictions for counseling the family and for rehabilitation or vocational planning. The third objective is to provide clinical data that can guide the treatment process by specifying both functional limitations and the processing strengths through which those limitations can be remediated. These two objectives may be best met by using nonstandardized clinical assessment tools that tap specific skills required for resumption of avocational and vocational interests and improved communicative interaction. Such data will be criterion-referenced and must be individualized to the specific needs and premorbid interests of each patient.

A final objective of evaluation, in some settings, may be further delineation of the behavioral manifestations of right hemisphere damage for research purposes. Here, assessment will depend on the nature and intent of a specific research design.

EVALUATION PROTOCOL

Test Profile

A test profile summary sheet that can be used as a cover sheet or attached to evaluation reports to provide a quick overview of the results of test administration is provided in Appendix 4–A. The profile sheet provides space for inclusion of scores received on each of the rating scales and tests, a checklist of other pertinent behaviors, and results of standardized testing. Initial test scores are recorded as well as data from two re-administrations of the test battery. Scores are reported as raw-score values relative to the total number of possible points. When one is using the test battery and reporting the scores, it is important to remember that ratings are scored relative to "adequacy" of performance rather than to a statistical norm. The scores cannot be used to evaluate vocational potential or make judgments about the patient's relative status compared with other adults who are the same age.

Behavioral Observation

Evaluation of the patient with right hemisphere damage begins with careful observation of general behavioral patterns and assessment of overall functional severity level. Initial behavioral observation is best conducted in several environmental settings to assess the impact of impairment within a variety of situational contexts:

- one-to-one interview in a quiet, nondistracting environment (i.e., patient's room with door closed and no other people present, or in a treatment room)
- one-to-one interview in a distracting environment (i.e., hospital waiting room or lounge)
- three-way interview with a family member or second professional

Behavioral Observation Profile

A behavioral observation profile is provided in Appendix 4–B. Interview questions and observational guidelines are included that may be used to probe behavioral functions. The following functions are assessed:

- attention
- eye contact
- awareness of illness
- orientation to place
- orientation to time
- orientation to person
- facial expression

- intonation
- topic maintenance

The profile is scored on a scale of 1 to 5 (see Appendix 4–B):

Attention. The ability to focus and sustain attention to stimuli is assessed. A patient would receive a score of *1* if unable to alert to his own name, attend to simple commands (he need not follow commands but should show awareness that performance is expected), or attend to a pointing task. A score of *3* would be assigned to the patient who attends to auditory stimuli some of the time but who is easily distracted by extraneous internal or external stimuli, has trouble shifting attention from one task to another, or impulsively responds to stimuli without waiting for completion of the stimulus and assessing all aspects of the situation. A score of *5* is given to a fully responsive patient.

Eye Contact. The patient's ability to focus initially on a speaker and use appropriate eye contact during conversation is assessed. Appropriate use of eye contact (*5*) includes using eye contact differently as the role changes from speaker to listener. For example, a speaker uses eye contact to evaluate the listener's interest in the topic, to establish role dominance, and as a turn-taking signal. A speaker need not maintain eye contact throughout a dialogue but can direct visual gaze to the left or right while thinking, for example; however, a listener is more bound to maintain eye contact with the speaker to show interest and signal agreement or disagreement. A score of *1* is given if the patient holds his head away from the other speaker and consistently looks at a fixed object or the far right visual field. A patient who is able to look toward the clinician when a conversation begins and when there is a change of turn but is unable to maintain eye contact to monitor the listener's interest in the topic would receive a score of *3*.

Awareness of Illness. The patient's awareness of the illness or specific deficits is assessed. The expected reaction to stroke or paralysis would be anger, depression, or sadness. An individual may have an optimistic outlook, even if somewhat unrealistic, but should be aware of present limitations relative to premorbid skills. Such a patient would receive a score of *5*. A patient would receive a score of *1* if expressing uncertainty about the cause of his illness or hospitalization and if he denies any obvious impairment such as hemiplegia, hemisensory deficit, or inability to read. Receiving a score of *3* would be the patient's descriptions of impairments that express uncertainty, such as "they tell me I have muscle weakness," or "I understand I had a stroke." Such a patient is likely to be aware of some major limitations but deny less obvious difficulties such as problems with calculation or understanding humor.

Orientation to Place. Passive and active orientation to place is assessed. A patient would receive a score of *1* if he is totally unaware of present location, such as a patient who tries to pay a hospital transporter for a taxi ride to treatment or who confuses the hospital with a hotel. A score of *3* would be given to the patient who expresses some confusion about his present location (i.e., thinking a move from one hospital ward to another represents a move to a new hospital) but has knowledge of basic orienting information. Such a patient will also usually show difficulty moving independently around the environment (active orientation), even in familiar surroundings. A score of *5* is reserved for the patient who is actively and passively oriented to place.

Orientation to Time. Knowledge of time concepts and the ability to monitor the passage of time is assessed. A patient would receive a score of *1* if unable to tell time or correctly identify or provide the day, date, year, or season. A score of *3* would be appropriate for the individual who can identify or provide some temporal information but has trouble with time concepts or monitoring the passage of time. A score of *5* is assigned to the patient who is actively and passively oriented to time.

Orientation to Person. The ability to recognize persons is assessed. To score this section, the clinician will need to rely on family and hospital staff reports as well as observation of the patient's responses on entering therapies or initial meetings with familiar persons. A patient would receive a score of *1* if family members report lack of recognition of immediate family or good friends. A score of *3* would be given to the patient who seems to rely heavily on paralinguistic cues (voice quality, evidence of a uniform) to recognize less familiar persons. Such a patient would probably show no evidence of recognition of a hospital staff member outside the hospital context. A score of *5* is given to the patient who easily recognizes family, friends, and new acquaintances, although he need not be able to remember names.

Facial Expression. Use of facial expression to show positive and negative emotion is assessed. Appropriate facial expression should not necessarily be obvious to another speaker but rather reflect the patient's general mood and attitude toward the conversational topic and listener. Such use of facial expression would be scored *5*. A patient who shows no alteration in facial posturing when told jokes or during verbal expressions of emotional states would receive a *1*. A patient with a generalized flat affect broken occasionally by an emotive expression of brief duration would receive a *3*, as would a patient who uses inappropriate expressions, such as expressions that draw attention to the speaker in inappropriate ways, do not accurately reflect the emotive content of a message, or detract from the patient's communication.

Intonation. Melodic contour of a speaker is assessed. The individual with an expressive aprosodia characteristically uses a stereotyped intonational contour that seems to have a droning quality. Prosody may be monotone, or it may simply lack the variation expected with differences in communicative intent. Such intonational contours would be scored a *1*. As with facial expression, a *3* would be given to the patient who shows either limited inflectional variation or who uses intonation inappropriately, such as making the voice very soft to shield communication inadequacies or talking too loudly in a library. Effective inflectional variation (*5*) should augment communication by signaling turn-taking routines, emphasizing new information in a dialogue, and maintaining interest in a narrative.

Topic Maintenance. The ability to maintain a topic during dialogue is assessed. An individual who is highly verbose, providing excessive detail or tangential digression, would receive a *1*, as would a person who does not answer questions directly or whose own choice of topic is vague or unclear most of the time. A patient who maintains the topic about 50% of the time would receive a *3*. The individual who maintains a topic over successive utterances or turns, clearly initiates topic changes at appropriate times, and signals such changes to the listener receives a *5*.

After computing the behavioral rating scale for a patient under three environmental conditions, the clinician should average the three scores to determine that patient's general severity rating. If the behavioral rating is performed in only one environmental condition, the clinician should describe the environment under which the severity rating was determined since even the patient with the mildest type of problem may show severe disturbances under conditions of competing noise or visual distraction.

Audiologic Assessment

In addition to a standard pure-tone evaluation of hearing acuity to rule out hearing loss as a factor in behavioral limitations, deficits in auditory attention and perception may be defined to some extent through audiologic assessment. A basic battery of hearing tests will reveal any sensory hearing loss, although unrelated to the stroke, that may be contributing to the patient's communicative problems. Having ruled out peripheral hearing loss, various tests of auditory discrimination, recognition, and memory may reflect damage to higher auditory association and processing centers.

Conversational word discrimination tests may be administered in a variety of controlled acoustic settings differing in signal intensity as well as in type and amount of distracting background noise. Beyond these, the tester may use formal and informal listening tasks that highlight the patient's ability or inability to discriminate differences in pitch, intensity, duration, and temporal patterning. These may be as simple as asking a listener whether two sound stimuli are the same or different. Auditory recognition ability for both verbal and nonverbal input may be assessed using sound–picture or sound–object association tasks. Measures of auditory memory span as well as auditory localization and tracking may be helpful in describing the ways in which the patient demonstrates poor auditory attention.

Visuoperceptual Testing

Visuoperceptual problems are a salient feature of the syndrome of right hemisphere damage and should be thoroughly evaluated as part of any diagnostic protocol. Visual skills should be specifically evaluated with the following objectives in mind (see Appendix 4–G for sources of tests):

1. Evidence of left hemianopia (clinical assessment)
2. Evidence of visual neglect of the left hemispace
   a. Within the environment (i.e., "Show me your left hand, right hand, left foot" and can the patient find you if you are seated on his left?)
   b. With printed verbal and nonverbal visual materials placed within the left visual field

3. Evidence of visuospatial deficits in tasks that do not require motoric response (*Motor-Free Visual Perception Test*)
4. Evidence of visuomotor disturbance (*Developmental Test of Visual-Motor Integration* and *Developmental Test of Visual Perception*)
5. Evidence of spatial orientation memory problems (*Spatial Orientation Memory Test*)
6. Evidence of visual scanning and tracking problems (Appendix 4–C)

Assessment of Language and Language-Related Skills

To rule out evidence of aphasia and to specify any possible language disturbances, all patients should receive a full language assessment (*Boston Diagnostic Aphasia Examination*).[18] By this point in the evaluation, the clinician should be aware of most of the major behavioral deficits exhibited by the patient. Further testing is therefore designed to probe individual skills more thoroughly in order to guide the therapeutic process and provide baseline measures. Assessment tools will be chosen according to deficits identified previously and based on the patient's own avocational and vocational objectives.

Reading

Standardized tests of reading should not be administered until a patient shows visuospatial and perceptual prerequisites. Deficits in these areas will preclude the ability to read for enjoyment or comprehension. Visuoperceptual deficits should be addressed as a separate therapeutic goal. As a general guideline, we suggest that the patient perform at an 8- to 9-year level on the *Motor-Free Visual Perceptual Test* or its equivalent and perform visual scanning and tracking tasks with 90% accuracy, demonstrating minimal reliance on verbal cuing. Reading comprehension batteries are most helpful for vocational counseling and as measures of recovery when they yield age or grade equivalency scores. Recommended batteries include *Gates-MacGinitie Reading Tests, Iowa Silent Reading Tests,* and *Woodcock Reading Mastery Tests.*

Writing

Written language and spelling measures are provided through administration of most standardized language tests for adult neurological populations. However, since patients with right hemisphere damage may show specific problems with spatial organization of writing, a rating scale specifically designed for use with this population has been developed. A short set of tasks designed to elicit the types of writing errors that typify this population is provided in Appendix 4–D. Task I requires copying a sentence that contains all the letters of the alphabet so that any poorly formed letters can be quickly identified. The second task requires spelling ten words to dictation. Care has been taken to include words of varying length, degree of phonetic spelling correspondence, and familiarity. Several words with double letters are included since patients with right hemisphere damage often experience difficulties with double letters. The final task requires a short written narrative of 100 words or more that can be used to evaluate the patient's spatial organization on the page, general legibility, and sentence composition skills. Each rating scale category is scored according to number or percent of errors and is coded for the writing task from which the score should be drawn.

Oral Expression

Pragmatics of communication includes conversational skills, use of paralinguistic cues to augment meaning, regulate meaning or emphasize some information over other, and use of context to convey information. These are now recognized as salient features of the syndrome of right hemisphere damage. (See Unit 3 for a review.) To the speech-language pathologist such communicative inadequacies are important to document so that family and medical staff can fully understand the potential limitations to vocational and avocational satisfaction after hospital discharge. Furthermore, such communication difficulties are often undetected in standardized cognitive appraisals but when documented provide another means of assessing recovery. Appendix 4–E has been developed to permit objective appraisal of a full range of pragmatic communication skills.

The *Scale of Pragmatic Communication Skills,* Appendix 4–E, is divided into four sections to provide separate measures of a patient's use of (A) nonverbal communication behaviors such as gestures and intonation; (B) conversational skills including ability to take turns, initiate conversation, and keep responses short and to the point; (C) ability to use linguistic context to maintain a topic, to judge how much information can be presupposed, and to refer backward or forward in a

conversation to other relevant information; and (D) ability of the patient to organize a complete narrative in retelling either a story or a joke. The rating scale should be scored according to the scoring criteria provided below:

Intonation. Scoring is the same as on the Behavioral Rating Scale.

Facial Expression. Scoring is the same as on the Behavioral Rating Scale.

Eye Contact. Scoring is the same as on the Behavioral Rating Scale.

Gestures and Proxemics. The patient's ability to use spontaneous gestures and changes in body posture to facilitate communication is assessed. A score of *5* would be given to the patient who uses gestures that signal meaning when verbal expression is less appropriate or useful, uses gestures and body posture to signal desire to take a turn, and uses gestures to emphasize important points in a conversation. As with facial expression, gestures should not draw attention away from other aspects of the conversation. A patient who uses inappropriate gestures or who uses only occasional vague or nonmeaningful gestures would receive a score of *3*. A score of *1* would be given to the patient who sits motionless throughout conversational interchanges.

Conversational Initiation. The ability to initiate conversations or topics within conversation is assessed. This area permits analysis of the patient's use of language to perform different functions (speech acts) either directly through the explicit meaning of an utterance or indirectly. Adequate conversational initiation is seen when an individual freely initiates a variety of speech acts, such as making requests, promises, or reminders and/or initiates new topics during a conversation. In other words the patient is seen as an "active" participant in a conversation. Such a conversant would receive a score of *5*. An individual who speaks only in response to another's questions, who provides little or no added information during a conversation, who initiates no topics, and/or whose speech acts are limited to answering would receive a score of *1*. The patient who is often a "passive" participant in the conversation but occasionally initiates a topic or makes a request would receive a score of *3*. The clinician is cautioned against rating an individual in this area based on an interview situation alone since such a conversational situation is conducive to limited variety in speech acts and restricts topic changes. It is suggested that observations of interactions with family members or staff be used.

Turn-taking. The ability to alternate conversational turns without interrupting or monopolizing a conversation is assessed. Adequate turn-taking skills necessitate detection of a listener's paralinguistic cues that he desires a turn, of ability to keep turns short enough to permit frequent, evenly distributed volleys between two participants, and of ability to signal the end of a turn or desire for a turn. Turn-taking signals are usually conveyed by gestures, changes in intonation, and alterations in eye contact and body posture. Appropriate use and responsiveness to signals is scored a *5*. A score of *1* is given when the individual seems totally unaware of the listener's signal to change turns and does not use content or cues to guide his own turn initiations or ends. Inconsistent ability to keep conversational volleys going would be scored a *3*.

Verbosity. The length of a patient's turns in dialogue is assessed. Appropriate turn length is determined by the intent of the utterance and the content. Generally an utterance should be long enough to clarify old information that is not presupposed within the context of the situation but should not contain redundant information or information irrelevant to the topic. When a patient's responses to questions stray from the topic and provide irrelevant or unnecessary information on a majority (over 50%) of turns, a score of *1* is given. When such utterances occur occasionally (25% to 50%) but do not characterize the patient's response pattern, a score of *3* is given. A score of *5* is given to the individual who maintains an adequate volley to maintain interest in the conversation. (Scoring of this area should be considered relative to the patient's premorbid tendencies as reported by family members since there is great variability in "talkativeness" among speakers.)

Topic Maintenance. The ability to address the point of a conversation is assessed. Topics should change in a dialogue as new information rendered on an old topic raises new questions and inspires comment. Adequate maintenance receives a score of *5*. When topics are changed more than one time within a turn, when the topic is unclear, or when comments are made that do not address the topic, topic maintenance is violated. Such violations occurring on more than 75% of the patient's utterances would yield a score of *1*. A score of *3* is given when the individual maintains the topic 50% of the time.

Presupposition. The ability to use shared knowledge between speaker and listener as a guide to how much information is explicitly verbalized is assessed. Effective communication is facilitated by omission of "common knowledge" and information that can be inferred from the context. A speaker who assumes too much of the listener leaves the listener unsure of the topic and content of his statements. A speaker who assumes too little gives the impression of "talking down" to the listener, with his content viewed as boring or too detailed. When either too much or too little presupposition occurs in over half of a person's turns a score of *1* is given. Occasional violation of presupposition (25% to 50%) receives a score of *3*. Adequate presupposition likely results in a rare uncertainty about the specifics of a topic or explicit reference to facts mutually understood (*5*). (Ability to presuppose varies with context and likely varies among individuals in different socioeconomic classes and professions; two lawyers might be expected to presuppose more than a carpenter when describing a legal action. Likewise, many persons provide more details about their jobs than about topics of less immediate interest.)

Referencing Skills. The ability to refer to objects and actions clearly and unambiguously is assessed. Referencing is inappropriate (*1*) when a speaker uses vague or improperly placed pronouns or other indefinites to refer to specific bits of information within a conversation, with the result that the meaning and/or intent of an utterance is unclear. Referencing can also be disturbed by using vague gestures or disorganized structural or temporal organization or by presupposing too much of the listener. A score of *3* would be given when a listener understands most of the content of a conversation without having to question or "query" to clarify unclear references. A score of *5* is reserved for conversations and narratives in which content is almost always clear and stated explicitly without resorting to redundancy.

Organization. The ability to organize discourse in a cohesive and clear manner is assessed. Disorganized narrative or discourse (*1*) is that in which temporal ordering of events and/or organization around a main theme are totally absent. The listener questions when, where, or why events occurred. Narratives in which details are ordered by time or in another linear fashion but that lack a unifying theme are scored *3*. Such narratives might provide extraneous details or irrelevant facts. A score of *5* is given to a well-told story in which the speaker provides only the information relevant to the main point of the story within a clear temporal or conceptual framework.

Completeness. The ability to specify all details required to make a point is assessed. A score of *1* would be given to a narrative in which salient details are missing or confabulations are evident in more than half of the content of the story. Omission or erroneous recall of 25% to 50% of the details would yield a score of *3*. A *5* would be given to complete rendering of a story or joke. (Note that completeness will vary depending on the length of a story or joke, complexity of the content, abstraction required, and familiarity with concepts. It is therefore recommended that the clinician use short anecdotes or jokes from materials designed for brain-damaged populations.)

In addition to analysis of pragmatic skills, assessment of high-level verbal expressive skills can be performed through use of *The Reporter's Test* and *The Visual–Verbal Test*. These tests are recommended to provide verification of severity of expressive disturbance and quantify pretreatment and post-treatment changes.

Memory

Problems with retention and retrieval are an additional component of many neurological syndromes and may be evident among patients with right hemisphere damage. Although memory testing is often thoroughly assessed as part of a neuropsychological test battery, clinicians may wish to evaluate specific retention/recall deficits as they specifically affect auditory comprehension, reading comprehension, and verbal expression. Clinical tools that may aid and/or augment neuropsychological testing of memory include *Detroit Tests of Learning Aptitude,* especially the subtests of "memory for designs," "auditory attention span for unrelated words," and "auditory attention span for related syllables," and the *Token Test.*

Integrative Skills

The literature also points to specific problems with high-level verbal reasoning and integrative skills in patients with right hemisphere lesions. Such problems necessitate attention, especially in evaluation of the patient with mild or minimal functional impairment, particularly if he plans to return to school or gainful employ-

ment. As with memory, neuropsychological test batteries often include assessment of integrative skills. Supplementary tests of value to the clinician that are specifically designed to assess integrative functions include *Ross Test of Higher Cognitive Processing, Detroit Tests of Learning Aptitude,* especially the subtests of "pictorial absurdities," "verbal absurdities," and "likenesses and differences," and *Watson-Glaser Critical Thinking Appraisal.* A list of common idioms and proverbs is provided in Appendix 4–F with a checklist for interpretation of the patient's explanations. Descriptions and sources of the tests mentioned previously are provided in Appendix 4–G.

The Metaphorical Language Test (see Appendix 4–F) contains ten idiomatic expressions that can be read aloud to the patient or that the patient can read aloud if oral reading skills are sufficiently intact. The patient is asked to explain each expression in his "own words." The clinician should check each response with respect to accuracy of interpretation as follows:

Literal interpretations are those in which each word is interpreted independent of the generalized context.
Examples:

1. Nothing attempted, nothing attained.
2. Watch out before you jump, there may be a big hole.
3. Sew it now and avoid a lot of sewing later.
4. He's part and parcel of the old block.
5. Save a penny and it's really like earning it.
6. It's coming down in animals.
7. Walk around and around the bush.
8. Save your money for when it rains or snows.
9. You'll be dirt to me.
10. It takes two people to dance.

Repeats or nearly repeats the phrase is similar to a paraphrase with only one or two words altered.
Examples:

1. Nothing ventured, nothing regained.
2. Look before you jump.
3. A stitch now saves nine.
4. He's a piece off from the old block.
5. A penny in the bank is a penny earned.
6. It's pouring cats and dogs.
7. Beat around the tree.
8. Save it for stormy times.
9. Your name will be dirt.
10. It takes two to tango at once.

Personal interpretations are those in which the metaphor is recognized only as it applies to the patient, especially past experiences.

Examples

1. If I don't try to get better, I won't.
2. That's my problem, I'm always tripping.
3. When my clothes are torn, they'll tear more if I wear them.
4. I look just like my father.
5. That's it, I can't save a dime, never could.
6. Like the storm in '72.
7. That's my brother Jack, you never know what he's getting at.
8. Yep and its raining right now, I'll tell you that.
9. That's what I told my kids when they fibbed.
10. Now that's the truth.

Partially correct responses often apply to the metaphor in an abstract way but contain errors or incorrect elaborations.

1. If you try something you might lose, but then you might not.
2. Before you head out into something, think about what the repercussions would be if you lost, it might be better not to try than to fail.
3. A stitch now may keep a disaster from occurring, like the little boy who held his finger in the flood wall and kept the town from going under.
4. Birds of a feather flock together.
5. Put a penny in the bank and soon it will earn compounded interest until first thing you know you'll have two cents or more.
6. It's raining lizards and lollipops, that's a down home expression where I come from.
7. Talk too much until everyone forgets the original question.
8. Don't spend your money because one day you'll need it to buy a raincoat for example.
9. People will think you're a fool.
10. Two people can get in trouble faster than one.

Perseverative responses are responses that are related to earlier items.

Normal abstract interpretations.
Examples:

1. You can't succeed if you don't try.
2. Think about the ramifications of your actions before making a move.
3. An ounce of prevention is worth a pound of cure.
4. The lad is just like his father.
5. When you save money you earn the right to spend it later.
6. It's pouring.
7. Doesn't get to the point.
8. Save something for when you really need it.
9. Your reputation will be ruined.
10. You can't fight without a partner.

Academic Skills

A final aspect of the evaluation of the patient with mild right hemisphere damage should include general assessment of academic and/or specific vocationally related skill areas. Foremost among these is assessment of calculation skills. Calculation disorders may be evident as an artifact of the visuoperceptual skills required for maintaining columns in calculation or keeping ledgers, as well as the perceptual and retention skills required for use of a calculator. Although true acalculia is rare in this population, integration skills required for verbal problem solving (e.g., algebra, calculus, geometry) are often impaired. Mathematical skills need only be assessed if the patient plans to use these skills at home or to return to a work environment or school setting where such skills would be required. Tests recommended for evaluation of mathematical skills include the Acalculia Subtest of the *Boston Diagnostic Aphasia Examination* and mathematical portions of the tests listed below.

Assessment of general areas of academic skills may be of value for vocational placement or return to school. Academic test batteries useful for such purposes and for guidance in therapeutic retraining include *Adult Basic Learning Examination* (ABLE), Levels I, II, and III, *Metropolitan Achievement Tests: High School Battery,* and *Stanford Achievement Test: High School Battery.*

REFERENCES

1. Hier DB, Mondlock J, Caplan LR: Behavioral abnormalities after right hemisphere stroke. *Neurology* 1983;33:337–344.

2. Foldi NS, Cicone M, Gardner H: Pragmatic aspects of communication in brain-damaged patients, in Segalowitz S (ed): *Language Functions and Brain Organization*. New York, Academic Press, 1983, pp 51–86.

3. Segalowitz S, Bryden MP: Individual differences in hemispheric representation of language, in Segalowitz S (ed): *Language Functions and Brain Organization*. New York, Academic Press, 1983, pp 341–372.

4. Millar JM, Whitaker HA: The right hemisphere's contribution to language: A review of the evidence from brain-damaged subjects, in Segalowitz S (ed): *Language Functions and Brain Organization*. New York, Academic Press, 1983, pp 87–114.

5. Gardner H, Brownell H, Wapner W, et al: Missing the point: The role of the right hemisphere in the processing of complex linguistic materials, in Perecman E (ed): *Cognitive Processing in the Right Hemisphere*. New York, Academic Press, 1983, pp 169–191.

6. Fisher CM: Disorientation to place. *Arch Neurol* 1982;39:33–36.

7. Burns M, Halper A, Mogil S: *Communication Problems in Right Hemispheric Brain Damage: Diagnostic and Treatment Approaches*. Chicago, Rehabilitation Institute of Chicago, 1983.

8. Myers P: Right hemisphere impairment, in Holland A (ed): *Language Disorders in Adults*. San Diego, College-Hill Press, 1984, pp 177–208.

9. Borod JC, Koff E, Caron HS: Right hemispheric specialization for the expression and appreciation of emotion: A focus on the face, in Perecman E (ed): *Cognitive Processing in the Right Hemisphere*. New York, Academic Press, 1983, pp 83–110.

10. Moscovitch M: The linguistic and emotional functions of the normal right hemisphere, in Perecman E (ed): *Cognitive Processing in the Right Hemisphere*. New York, Academic Press, 1983, pp 57–82.

11. Ross ED, Mesulam M: Dominant language functions of the right hemisphere. *Arch Neurol* 1979;36:144–148.

12. Bryden MP, Ley RG: Right hemispheric involvement in imagery and affect, in Perecman E (ed): *Cognitive Processing in the Right Hemisphere*. New York, Academic Press, 1983, pp 111–124.

13. Riege WH, Metter EJ, Hanson WR: Verbal and non-verbal recognition memory in aphasic and nonaphasic stroke patients. *Brain Lang* 1980;10:60–70.

14. Whitehouse PJ: Imagery and verbal encoding in left and right hemisphere damaged patients. *Brain Lang* 1981;14:315–332.

15. Caramazza A, Gordon J, Zurirf EB, DeLuca D: Right-hemisphere damage and verbal problem solving behavior. *Brain Lang* 1976;3:41–46.

16. Winner E, Gardner H: The comprehension of metaphor in brain damaged patients. *Brain* 1977;100:717–729.

17. Gardner H, Ling K, Flamm L, et al: Comprehension and appreciation of humor in brain damaged patients. *Brain* 1975;93: 399–412.

18. Goodglass H, Kaplan E: *The Assessment of Aphasia and Related Disorders*. Philadelphia, Lea & Febiger, 1983.

RIC Evaluation of Communication Problems in Right Hemisphere Dysfunction (RICE)

by Martha S. Burns, Ph.D., CCC-SP, Anita S. Halper, M.A., CCC-SP
and Shelley I. Mogil, M.S., CCC-SP

Test Profile

Patient's Name _____ Clinician _____

	SCORES		
	Initial Test (Date _____)	*Re-test* (Date _____)	*Re-test* (Date _____)
I. General Behavioral Patterns			
A. Behavioral observation profile			
Environment:			
Quiet, one-to-one	/45	/45	/45
Noisy, one to one	/45	/45	/45
Three-way conversation	/45	/45	/45
B. Severity rating			
C. Other pertinent behaviors (check if present):			
Impulsivity			
Perseveration			
Unaware of errors			
Lack of task orientation			
Unable to self-correct errors			
Neglect of left hemispace			
Other (specify)			
II. Visual Scanning and Tracking			
A. Subtest #1			
Number of errors			
Time			

	SCORES		
	Initial Test	*Re-test*	*Re-test*
B. Subtest #2			
Number of errors	_____	_____	_____
Time	_____	_____	_____
C. Subtest #3			
Number of errors	_____	_____	_____
Time	_____	_____	_____
D. Subtest #4			
Number of errors	_____	_____	_____
Time	_____	_____	_____
III. Assessment and Analysis of Writing Errors	/55	/55	/55
IV. Assessment of Pragmatic Communication Violations	/60	/60	/60
V. Metaphorical Language	/10	/10	/10
VI. Other Tests Administered			
Tests:			
_____	_____	_____	_____
_____	_____	_____	_____
_____	_____	_____	_____

VII. Comments:

Appendix 4–B

Behavioral Observation Profile

A. Interview Questions (to be used as a guide to probe behavioral functions):

1. What is your name? Address?

2. Where are you right now? (Are you in the hospital?)

3. Why are you here? (Did you have a stroke? Are you having problems walking?)

4. How long have you been here? (When were you admitted? When did you become ill?)

5. What is the date today? (What is the day, month, year?)

6. What time is it?

7. What is your occupation?

8. What specific problems are you having now? (Can you read and write? Have you tried since you became ill? Are you having problems identifying your family or friends when they visit?)

9. Have you eaten today? (What meals have you eaten today? How is the food here?)

10. Have your family or friends been here to visit you?

11. Do you know who I am?

12. Can you show me where your television, telephone, night table, wash basin, closet, etc., are?

13. How long would you say you have been here with me?

B. Observations

1. Observe patient in interactions with family members and hospital staff to determine orientation to person.

2. Observe patient's ability to find the way from nursing station to own room to determine active orientation to place.

Rehabilitation Institute of Chicago Evaluation

C.   Scoring

	1	2	3	4	5
Attention	Inattentive		Attentive and Responsive part of the time (50%)		Fully Responsive
Eye Contact	None		At times		Appropriate
Awareness of Illness	Denies illness or hemiplegia		Aware of some problems but not others		Fully Aware
Orientation to place (family report and obser- vation)	Unaware of present location		Passive orientation to place but cannot find way around environment		Oriented
Orientation to time	Unaware of date, time, day, season		Passive orientation to time but unable to monitor passage of time		Oriented
Orientation to person (family report and obser- vation)	Confuses family and friends		Knows highly familiar people		Oriented
Facial Expression	None		Limited or inappropriate		Appropriate
Intonation	Flat or stereotyped		Limited or inappropriate		Appropriate
Topic Maintenance	Maintains topic less than 25% of the time		Maintains topic 50% of the time		Maintains topic

Total

Quiet _____
Noisy _____
3-Way _____
Average _____

Note: Color code each rating to distinguish different environments.

Rehabilitation Institute of Chicago Evaluation
Copyright © 1985 by Aspen Systems Corporation

D. Severity Rating

Total	*Description*
9–15	*Severe* Patient has severe deficits in attention, orientation, and communication interaction.
16–23	*Moderately Severe* Patient has marked deficits in attention, orientation, and/or communication interaction but responds appropriately to some simple stimuli.
24–31	*Moderate* Patient has functional communication in simple familiar contexts, responding appropriately to most simple stimuli but continuing to show problems with attention, eye contact, denial, orientation, and/or affect.
32–39	*Mild* Patient appears to function adequately in most situations, but specific impairments become apparent in distracting settings or through structured assessment.
40–45	*Minimal to Normal* Patient communicates in full range of contexts although subtle deficits in integrative skills persist.

Visual Scanning and Tracking

Subtest #1: (Total letters **85**; target letters **21**)
Scanning for large, widely spaced letters

Number of errors _____
Time _____

FFF	F	R	T	A	F	G	E	F	V	D	F	J	U	I	K	O	F
FFF	T	R	A	F	E	F	D	S	F	B	G	E	F	D	C	M	N
FFF	F	R	G	U	T	F	V	C	A	D	F	C	E	O	P	F	H
FFF	D	E	F	G	V	B	N	M	U	I	F	X	W	F	E	T	H
FFF	T	G	U	F	D	S	F	X	Z	Q	E	F	V	F	M	O	F

Subtest #2: (Total letters **305**; target letters **51**)
Scanning for small, closely spaced letters

Number of errors _____
Time _____

aaaa ieypeakziwqlakekakrhamwoaneialfjeaqoekfjaieuwkaoqpwoeiakfjrud

bbbb peoqbdjfubejhkrjbhaubdkejgyblskfirhtjbsjeugybdjehblapeigbhgjt

cccc elckeicdjecdyeuqicflgkhjcrgtufycdjghtocldkghtcoejgucdhejcdkrh

dddd eidelcidsjedcjehgrdcorituyjhkghqpeotdmcnvbghdoeiruydkaedjdmen

eeee fielecieoelcdeoqueciskechqjeurkrjeoxrpskalepwoeifjtheithfjeog

Subtest #3: (Total letters **28**; target letters **8**)
Scanning for large, widely spaced words

Number of errors _____
Time _____

MATCH	FETCH	HALF	MATH	MATCH	HATCH	MATCH	RETCH
ROUND	SOUND	FOUND	SOUND	HOUND	ROUND	FOUND	ROUND
HARD	HALF	PATH	HARD	HAND	FAND	HARD	CARD
RADIO	RIDE	RODEO	RODEO	VICE	RADIO	VIDEO	RADIO

Rehabilitation Institute of Chicago Evaluation

Subtest #4: (Total letters **90**; target letters **43**)   Number of errors _____
Scanning for small, closely spaced words   Time   _____

the	hte	the	eth	the	then	the	hte	the	tle	the	teh	hte	the	ten	the
sit	tis	sit	sil	sit	cit	sit	sit	til	tis	sit	sil	sit	sid	sit	sit
let	led	del	let	ted	let	det	let	let	lel	tel	let	. ted	let	let	tel
can	can	cat	dan	can	nan	nac	can	can	cam	can	nac	can	cat	can	nat
tip	tip	pit	pid	tip	tip	tid	tib	tip	dip	tip	tid	tip	tid	tip	pit
her	her	ter	hen	her	ber	her	hed	her	reh	hen	hem	her	ter	her	her

Rehabilitation Institute of Chicago Evaluation

Tasks for Assessment and Analysis of Writing

On separate sheet of unlined paper:

A. Have the patient copy the following alphabetically balanced sentence:

The quick brown fox jumps over the lazy dog.

B. Dictate the following words:

> **phone**
>
> **saw**
>
> **ramp**
>
> **butter**
>
> **chimney**
>
> **insist**
>
> **little**
>
> **annual**
>
> **coloring**
>
> **January**

C. Have the patient write a description of an action picture, a description of a recent event, or a letter to a friend or family member. (Try to elicit a sample of at least 100 words.)

Rehabilitation Institute of Chicago Evaluation

D.   Scoring

	1	2	3	4	5
Visuospatial Disorganization (superimposed letters and lines and lines progressing on a diagonal)*	Always present (100%)		Present part of the time (50%)		Adequate
Left-sided Neglect (writing begins to right of appropriate left-hand margin)*	Always		Part of the time or center placement		Not Present
Omissions of Letters*	30 or more omissions		15 omissions		Less than 3 omissions
Omission of Strokes (e.g., unclosed *a*s and *o*s, *i*s undotted, *t*s uncrossed, etc.)*	100 or more omissions		50 omissions		Less than 10 omissions
Perseveration of Strokes and/or Letters*	30 or more		Less than 15		Less than 3
Ambiguous Sentences†	50% or more of sentences unclear		25% or more of sentences unclear		One or less unclear sentence
Run-on Sentences†	Always present (100%)		Present part of the time (50%)		Not present
Incomplete Sentences†	Always present (100%)		Present part of the time (50%)		Not present
Grammatical Errors†	(10)		(5)		One or none
Phonetically Based Spelling Errors‡	80% or more		40%		Correct
Visually Based Spelling Errors‡	80% or more		40%		Correct

*Score from writing tasks A, B, and C (Appendix 4–C).   Total _____
†Score from writing task C (Appendix 4–C).
‡Score from writing task B (Appendix 4–C).

Rehabilitation Institute of Chicago Evaluation
Copyright © 1985 by Aspen Systems Corporation

Appendix 4–E

Rating Scale of Pragmatic Communication Skills

A. Nonverbal Communication

	1	2	3	4	5
Intonation	Flat or stereotyped		Limited or inappropriate		Appropriate
Facial Expression	None		Limited or inappropriate		Appropriate
Eye Contact	Cannot establish or maintain eye contact		Needs cues to establish or maintain eye contact		Appropriate
Gestures and Proxemics	Inappropriate or does not use		Inconsistent appropriate use		Appropriate

B. Conversational Skills

	1	2	3	4	5
Conversational Initiation	Inappropriate or does not initiate		Inconsistent appropriate initiation		Appropriate

Rehabilitation Institute of Chicago Evaluation

	1	2	3	4	5
Turn-taking	Does not obey signals		Inconsistently responsive to signals		Adequate
Verbosity	Over 50% of responses are verbose or tangential		25% to 50% of responses are verbose or tangential		Appropriate response length

C. Use of Linguistic Context

	1	2	3	4	5
Topic Maintenance	Maintains topic less than 25% of the time		Maintains topic 50% of the time		Maintains topic
Presupposition	Presupposes too much and/or too little 50%		Presupposes too much and/or too little 25% to 50%		Appropriate
Referencing Skills	Inappropriate referencing		Inconsistent appropriate referencing		Appropriate

D. Organization of a Narrative

	1	2	3	4	5
Organization	Disorganized		Some organization but lacks a unifying theme		Adequate
Completeness	More than 50% of details are missing and/or inaccurate		25% to 50% of details are missing or inaccurate		Adequate

E. Assessment and Explanation of Terms

I. Assessment: Pragmatic communication skills should be assessed from a dialogue between the clinician and patient in as ''natural'' a manner as possible. For example, the patient can be interviewed about topics of interest in an informal setting rather than a testing situation. Discourse organization should be scored from a narrative summary such as retelling a joke or short story in addition to the dialogue.

Rehabilitation Institute of Chicago Evaluation

II. Explanation of Terms:
   a.   Nonverbal Communication:
        1. Intonation—melodic contour, score as in Appendix 4–B.
        2. Facial Expression—score as in Appendix 4–B.
        3. Eye Contact—eye contact of a listener should be directed toward the speaker most of the time; as a speaker, eye contact is established at the beginning and end of the turn.
        4. Gestures and Proxemics—conversants should remain a comfortable distance apart, changing body posture/position and gesturing to emphasize new information and maintain the listener's interest.
   b.   Conversational Postulates:
        1. Conversational Initiation—ability to initiate a conversation or new topic
        2. Turn-taking—responding to nonverbal turn-taking cues such as dropping intonational contour, pausing, and reestablishing eye contact
        3. Verbosity—tendency to overexpound on a topic
   c.   Linguistic Context:
        1. Topic Maintenance—score as in Appendix 4–B
        2. Presupposition—ability to omit redundant information or information already known to both conversants.
        3. Referencing Skills (anaphora and cataphora)—appropriate use of pronouns or other references to previous information within a dialogue (anaphora) or upcoming information within a dialogue (cataphora), such as, ''I will make three points . . . one . . . two . . . three . . .'', etc.
   d.   Discourse Organization:
        1. Organization—ability to organize a joke or story logically and/or temporally with a clearly stated unifying theme
        2. Completeness—ability to provide adequate or correct details in a joke or story summary

Metaphorical Language Test

Have the patient explain the following proverbs and idioms from an auditory stimulus.
Check response category applicable to each item.

	Completely Incorrect	Literal Interpretation	Repeats or Nearly Repeats the Phrase	Personal Interpretation	Partially Correct	Perseverative Response	Normal Abstract Interpretation
1. Nothing ventured, nothing gained.							
2. Look before you leap.							
3. A stitch in time saves nine.							
4. He's a chip off the old block.							
5. A penny saved is a penny earned.							
6. It's raining cats and dogs.							
7. Beat around the bush.							
8. Save it for a rainy day.							
9. Your name will be mud.							
10. It takes two to tango.							

Total correct _____

Rehabilitation Institute of Chicago Evaluation

Diagnostic Materials

VISUAL PERCEPTION

Developmental Test of Visual-Motor Integration by Keith E. Beery and Norman A. Buktenica (1967). Follett Publishing Co., 110 W. Washington Blvd., Chicago, IL 60607.
- Measures integration between visual perception and motor behavior. Raw score conversion to age equivalents are available within an age range of 3 to 16 years.

Developmental Test of Visual Perception by Marianne Frostig and Associates (1966). Consulting Psychologists Press, Inc., 577 College Ave., Palo Alto, CA 94306.
- Measures five component skills of visual perception: (1) eye–motor coordination, (2) figure–ground perception, (3) constancy of shape, (4) position in space, and (5) spatial relationships. Raw score conversion to age equivalent scores, scaled scores, and percentile ranks are available for children only.

Motor-Free Visual Perception Test by Ronald P. Colarusso and Donald D. Hammill (1972). Academic Therapy Publications, 20 Commercial Blvd., Novato, CA 94947.
- Measures five areas of visual perception (spatial relationships, visual discrimination, figure–ground, visual closure, and visual memory) and requires no graphic responses. Mean raw score values are provided for ages 4 to 9 years and 18 to 80 years.

Revised Visual Retention Test, 4th edition, by Arthur Benton (1974). The Psychological Corporation, 757 Third Ave., New York, NY 10017.
- Assesses visual perception, visual memory, and visuoconstructive abilities through reproduction of designs. Ratings and IQ equivalents for children and adults are available.

Spatial Orientation Memory Test by Joseph M. Wepman and Dainis Turaids (1975). Western Psychological Services, Order Dept., 12031 Wilshire Blvd., Los Angeles, CA 90025.
- Measures visual retention and recall of the spatial orientation of forms. Mean raw score values are provided for ages 5 to 10 years.

LANGUAGE-RELATED ACADEMIC TESTS

Adult Basic Learning Examination (ABLE): Levels I, II, and III by Bjorn Karlsen, Richard Madden, and Eric Gardner (1971). The Psychological Corporation, 757 Third Ave., New York, NY 10017.
- Measures auditory vocabulary, reading comprehension of sentences and paragraphs, reading comprehension of news items (Level III only), spelling, and arithmetic computations and problem solving. Grade equivalents are available

for Levels I (grades 1–6) and II (grades 3–9). Stanine and percentile equivalents are available for Level III (grades 9–12).

Detroit Tests of Learning Aptitude by Harry J. Baker and Bernice Leland (1967). Pro-Ed, 5341 Industrial Oaks Blvd., Austin, TX 78735.
- Includes subtests on pictorial absurdities, verbal absurdities, auditory attention span for unrelated words, social adjustment, orientation, memory for designs, auditory attention span for related syllables, and likenesses and differences. Raw score conversions to age equivalency scores are available for ages 3 to 19 years.

Gates-MacGinitie Reading Tests: Survey D, E, F, 2nd edition, by Walter H. MacGinitie and Associates (1978). The Riverside Publishing Co., 8420 Bryn Mawr Ave., Chicago, IL 60631.
- Measures reading vocabulary and comprehension. Survey D has norms available for grades 4 through 6. Survey E has norms available for grades 7 through 9. Survey F has norms available for grades 10 through 12. Percentile ranks, stanines, and grade equivalents are available for grades 4 through 12.

Iowa Silent Reading Tests: Levels 1, 2, 3, Roger Farr, ed. (1973). The Psychological Corporation, 757 Third Ave., New York, NY 10017.
- Level 1 measures vocabulary, reading comprehension, and directed reading. Level 2 measures vocabulary, reading comprehension, directed reading, and reading efficiency. Level 3 measures vocabulary, reading comprehension, and reading efficiency. Percentile ranks, stanine scores, and standard scores are available for grades 6 through 12 and college students.

Metropolitan Reading Instructional Tests: Elementary, Intermediate, and Advanced I by Roger Farr, George A. Prescott, Irving H. Balow, and Thomas P. Hogan (1978). The Psychological Corporation, 757 Third Ave., New York, NY 10017.
- Elementary level measures matching a word to an auditory stimulus, identification of initial consonants, matching vowel sounds, vocabulary in context, word part clues, reading comprehension, and rate of comprehension. Intermediate level measures identification of initial consonants, matching vowel sounds, vocabulary in context, word part clues, skimming and scanning, reading comprehension, and rate of comprehension. Advanced I level

measures vocabulary in context, skimming and scanning, reading comprehension, and rate of comprehension. Scaled score conversions for grade equivalents, stanines, and percentile ranks are available for grades 3 through 10.

Reporter's Test by E. DeRenzi and C. Ferrari (1978). A sensitive test to detect expressive disturbances in aphasics. *Cortex* 1978; 14:279–293.
- Tests ability to produce connected sequences of words by requiring the patient to report actions orally that the examiner is performing. These performances correspond, for the most part, to the commands of the *Token Test.* Mean raw scores and weighted scores for normal individuals, aphasics, and adults with right hemisphere damage are provided.

Ross Test of Higher Cognitive Processes by John D. Ross and Catherine M. Ross (1976). Academic Therapy Publications, 20 Commercial Blvd., Novato, CA 94947.
- Assesses abstract and critical thinking skills, including analysis, synthesis, and evaluation. Raw score means are provided for gifted and normal students in grades 4 through 6.

Stanford Achievement Test—Listening Comprehension Test: Intermediate I, II, Advanced by Eric F. Gardner, Herbert C. Rudman, Bjorn Karlsen, and Jack C. Merwin (1982). The Psychological Corporation, 757 Third Ave., New York, NY 10017.
- Evaluates ability to retain details and organize content of orally presented information. Percentile ranks, scaled scores, grade equivalents, and stanines through grade 10 are provided.

Token Test by E. DeRenzi and L.A. Vignolo (1962). A sensitive test to detect receptive disturbances in aphasics. *Brain* 1962; 85:665–678.
- Tests ability to comprehend auditorily, retain, and follow progressively more complex oral commands having minimal redundancy. The test is standardized on normal individuals and aphasics.

Visual-Verbal Test by Marvin J. Feldman and James Drasgow (1981). Western Psychological Services, Order Dept., 12031 Wilshire Blvd., Los Angeles, CA 90025.
- Tests ability to abstract conceptual similarities on a verbal level and to shift from one conceptual set to another. The test is standardized on a normal and brain-damaged population.

Rehabilitation Institute of Chicago Evaluation

Watson-Glaser Critical Thinking Appraisal by Goodwin Watson and Edward M. Glaser (1980). The Psychological Corporation, 757 Third Ave., New York, NY 10017.
- Tests ability to make inferences, recognize assumptions, make deductions, draw conclusions, and evaluate arguments from written stimuli. Percentile scores are available for adolescents and adults.

Woodcock Reading Mastery Tests by Richard Woodcock (1973). American Guidance Service, Publisher's Building, Circle Pines, MN 55014.
- Measures letter and word identification, word attack, and word and passage comprehension. Provides raw score conversion to easy reading level, reading grade score, and failure reading level for grades 1 through 12.

Treatment of Communication Problems in Right Hemisphere Damage

Martha S. Burns, Ph.D., CCC-SP, Anita S. Halper, M.A., CCC-SP, and
Shelley I. Mogil, M.S., CCC-SP

A treatment hierarchy with specific goals, procedures, and measurements designed for the patient with right hemisphere damage is presented in this unit. To use this hierarchy effectively several treatment issues unique to this population must be considered. In addition, education and counseling of family members and staff is an integral part of the treatment program.

EDUCATION AND COUNSELING OF FAMILY AND STAFF

Little information about the nature and extent of right hemisphere lesions is available to the general public. It is essential that the patient's family and hospital staff be instructed about the nature of the patient's limitations and expected course of recovery. The family and staff particularly should be made aware of such features of the syndrome as *denial of deficits, impulsivity, place and time disorientation,* and *problems with judgment and reasoning.* Many patients will also exhibit *lack of affect,* which results in an apparent disinterest in personal interactions. Deficits in *visuospatial perception* should be explained in terms of the effect on physical maneuvering, orientation, and reading and writing. *Altered body concept* is likely to affect activities of daily living.

If the above deficits are not clearly explained in the initial stages of treatment, it has been our experience that families may attribute many features of right hemisphere disorders to personality or emotional changes. Similarly, the staff may misinterpret some of these behaviors as signs of rejection or disinterest rather than a disruption in the ability for communicative interaction. The clinician should assure that other staff and family members anticipate dangers to the patient caused by impulsivity and/or visuospatial imperception.

Family members and significant others are essential members of the treatment team. Goals should be mutually developed by the patient, family, and clinician. The patient's premorbid educational level, skills, and interests should be considered when setting therapeutic objectives and developing procedures. The family will need to be taught how and when to rely on verbal mediation strategies to help the patient compensate for processing deficits. Incorporation of the family into the therapeutic process at all stages will also help the family and patient adjust to the illness and maximize carryover. Guidelines for communication management for family members and hospital staff are provided in Appendix 5–A, and a detailed discussion of family involvement and support is provided in Unit 6.

TREATMENT ISSUES

Perhaps unlike any other type of neurological disorder of communication, treatment of right hemisphere disorders is fraught with continual frustrations to both patient and clinician. Much of the frustration stems from uncertainty about the specific nature of the disturbances themselves. There are also treatment issues peculiar to this population that if not considered as part of the treatment regimen, can severely undermine the therapeutic process.

Prior to enrolling a patient in an organized treatment program, the clinician must determine his readiness for organized instruction. As is true with any neurologically impaired person, the patient should be medically stable, physically able to tolerate sitting upright in bed or a chair for a minimum of 15 minutes, aware of the external environment, and responsive to external stimuli. Severe attentional disturbances are common in this population and need not preclude initiation of treatment as long as the patient is able to alert to auditory and/or tactile stimuli, even if only for brief periods. Alerting to visual stimuli may take longer to resolve in this population owing to the severe visuospatial impairments that typify right hemisphere damage. It has been our experience that patients with right hemisphere lesions reach these criteria within a few days post onset, while individuals with bilateral involvement may remain unresponsive to external stimuli for much longer periods of time.

Problems with attention and retention are salient features of right hemisphere disorder and persist throughout recovery. Even in the mildest forms of the disorder, patients may exhibit an intolerance for extraneous noise or a visually complex environmental activity, such as crowds or even television. They may show problems concentrating on even the most routine tasks in noisy or visually busy settings. Because of this, at all levels of treatment, clinicians will likely find it necessary to control the patient's impulsivity and to control the therapeutic environment by manipulating the amount of competing stimuli. The therapeutic hierarchy provided in this unit begins with developing basic attentional skills; however, because of the pervasiveness of attentional disturbances, one goal of treatment at all procedural levels should include increasing the patient's ability to focus, shift, and/or sustain attention to that task. To accomplish this, task formats should include shifts in input and output modalities. As the amount of competing stimuli, complexity of the task, and the task format are varied, response time on a specific task will also vary. In some cases improvement will reflect an increase in response time and in some cases a decrease.

At advanced levels of treatment, clinicians may find themselves repeatedly arguing with a patient about the best interpretation of a logic or reasoning task. This is most likely to occur if treatment levels are advanced too rapidly. For that reason, we have developed a hierarchy of treatment goals to provide maximum practice with tasks at each processing level. The more highly systematized the therapeutic hierarchy is, the more easily the patient will be able to course through the treatment program. However, the clinician should be careful to adapt levels and materials to the specific needs and interests of each patient, modifying goals and procedures as necessary.

Often clinicians express concern over the value of treating a patient who does not recognize or is unconcerned about his deficits. The patient's denial of deficit can be controlled somewhat by careful organization of treatment goals and task levels. In addition, it is essential with the right hemisphere–disordered population that clinicians be especially cautious about establishing clear goals with the patient and family. Prior to initiating any new phase of treatment, the clinician should objectively measure change in a way that the patient can see and understand. In some cases, the benefits to be gained from treatment will not outweigh the patient's frustration and desire to terminate therapy.

TREATMENT HIERARCHY

With the previous issues in mind, this section of the manual provides a carefully structured hierarchy of treatment goals with corresponding procedures and measurement guidelines. Goals have been organized according to general level of severity rather than by modality or task. Many characteristics of right hemisphere disorders do not seem to be modality or task specific but rather manifestations of attention, retention, and gestalt perceptual/reasoning breakdowns. The exception to this would be the visuospatial perceptual tasks that are specifically geared to a modality disturbance.

Within the hierarchy of severity level, it is useful to subcategorize the goals according to purported primary processing capabilities (i.e., attention, retention, orientation, and/or integration). This organization is a purely superficial one, since goals and tasks at all levels require a full range of processing. Concentrating on even the most routine tasks in noisy or visually confusing settings requires attentional focus, retention of directions, and integration of input and output modalities. On high-level symbolic reasoning tasks, patients may need assistance with focusing and maintaining attention. The clinician may also need to structure the environment to maximize attentional skills. The processing levels, then, should not be thought of as clear-cut divisions but rather processing capabilities that must be considered at each level of performance.

Accordingly, the treatment hierarchy is meant as a guide, not an exhaustive list, for retraining skills through education, cuing, facilitation, and so on.

Examples of specific treatment, measurement materials, and an annotated bibliography of commercially available treatment materials appear in Appendixes 5–B and 5–C.

Attention

The primary goal at this level is to increase gradually the patient's attentional skills, not to strive for correct answers. Therefore, at all levels of treatment the clinician should begin with an easy, non-frustrating task and increase complexity slowly while maintaining the achieved level of attention. Clinical activities are organized to increase the patient's ability to *focus* attention to the task, to *shift* attentional set from one modality to another or from task to task, and to *sustain* attention for longer periods of time.[1]

Goal	Procedure	Measurement
1. Focus attention to task in a sterile environment:		
a. Establish eye contact with speaker	Physically manipulate patient's head, use verbal cues, and/or gesture to establish eye contact with clinician.	Percent of times head must be manipulated and/or number of cues required to reestablish eye contact per designated time period
	Use exaggerated inflection or gesture to maintain eye contact.	Same as above
b. Establish visual gaze to treatment activity	Physically manipulate patient's head, use verbal cues, and/or gesture to establish gaze to task.	Same as above
c. Establish pointing response to treatment activity	Physically manipulate patient's hand, use verbal cues, and/or gesture to establish pointing response. Have patient point to: • Large colored dots. • Family pictures. • Environmental objects.	Number of cues required to establish pointing response and/or number of pointing responses with and without cues
d. Shift eye contact from treatment activity to a speaker	Call patient's name or have patient paged on loudspeaker periodically during a task.	Percent of correct responses to name and number of cues required
2. Focus attention to task in an environment with competing stimuli:		
a. Establish eye contact with speaker	Introduce the following competing stimuli while attempting to get the patient to attend to his name or localize to speech: • Turn on radio in background. • Open door to hall. • Take patient outside treatment area.	Percent correct and length of time required to establish eye contact
b. Establish visual gaze and pointing response to treatment activity	Use pointing tasks with above auditory competing stimuli and/or visual competing stimuli (e.g., books on the table or pictures on the wall).	Percent of correct pointing responses and length of time required per number of items
3. Shift attentional set	Vary input modes. Choose a task (see Example #1 in Appendix 5–B) at patient's perceptual and memory level; shift from requiring visual input only to visual/auditory input to auditory only.	Percent of appropriate shifts and length of time required to change attentional set
	Vary stimulus materials. Use above tasks; shift from one stimulus type (e.g., color) to another (e.g., size).	Same as above

Goal	Procedure	Measurement
	Vary response requirements. Use above tasks; shift from one response mode (e.g., pointing) to another (e.g., underlining) with same stimuli.	Same as above
4. Shift attention from task to nontask	Choose a task at patient's perceptual and memory level, and gradually increase number of times where shift is required, as below: • Initiate rest periods by asking patient to stop and return to task. • Introduce controlled interruptions (e.g., phone ring) or conversational aside.	Length of time taken for shift and/or type and number of cues required to make a shift
5. Shift attention from speaker to speaker	Bring a second person into the session (e.g., family member or another patient); initiate a dialogue requiring patient to establish eye contact with each new speaker: • Use exaggerated vocal inflection or gestures to assist patient in making shift. • Decrease gradually the use of exaggerated cues. • Decrease gradually the length of each speaker's turn to increase number of shifts required per session.	Number of attention shifts per designated time period and/or number of cues required per shift
	Use above hierarchy in group treatment activities.	Same as above
6. Sustain attention to task	All levels of treatment activities	Note time activity was initiated and times patient stopped attending and required refocusing throughout a treatment session or task.

Orientation

Orientation skills depend on memory.[1,2] Orientation to *place, time,* and *situation* will first need to be developed *passively*. Here, the emphasis will be on the patient's recognition of familiar personal belongings, time of day, and so on. As the patient demonstrates ability to focus on salient features of his environment and to recognize time and place, treatment will shift to *active* orientation. At this stage, emphasis will be on using orientation skills to regain independence in moving around the hospital and following schedules. Orientation to *person* is often not a goal with this population because patients seem to compensate readily for facial recognition deficits (prosopagnosia).

To decrease the patient's impulsivity on passive orientation tasks, the patient must be instructed to scan the entire environment for relevant details, rather than draw conclusions based on one stimulus item. In active orientation tasks, the patient will need to be reminded to survey the environment passively prior to initiating activities.

Goal	Procedure	Measurement
1. Establish knowledge of basic biographical/environmental information	Impart a select core of information (see Example #2 in Appendix 5–B) to patient using visual supplements as appropriate (e.g., calendar)	
	• Have patient repeat facts immediately.	Number of stimulus repetitions required to obtain accurate response
	• Repeat facts after a brief delay.	Same as above
	• Provide facts after interference with other orientation facts.	Percent of correct facts provided
	• Provide facts after intervening tasks.	Same as above
	Increase gradually the number of items in the core using above procedures.	Use above measures as appropriate
	Begin each session with patient providing above information as appropriate; retrain on items in error.	Percent of correct facts provided
2. Establish orientation to person	Present simultaneously photographs and brief audio recordings (if possible) of significant others; have patient name. Use visual cues such as age, sex, or other distinctive features (see Example #3 in Appendix 5–B).	Percent of correct responses
	Present above photographs without recordings; build visual self-cuing techniques.	Percent of correct responses
	Present photographs of nonfamiliar persons and discuss use of visual self-cuing techniques for recognition (see Example #3).	Percent of self-generated versus clinician-generated cues
3. Establish passive orientation to place	Present familiar objects from the patient's environment; use verbal association cues to facilitate recognition of rooms in which these objects are found.	Percent of correct room identifications
	Present pictures of rooms and follow above procedure.	Same as above
	Present pictures of buildings and follow above procedures.	Percent of correct building identifications

Goal	Procedure	Measurement
4. Establish passive orientation to time		
a. Telling time of day, date, day of week, season, day versus night	Present temporal aids (e.g., pocket calendar, daily log). Use these aids to cue recognition of time factors. (See also ''Memory Books'' under ''Memory'' section.)	Percent of correct responses
b. Telling time	Use clear blank large-face watch or digital watch: • Affix strip of red tape or bells to alert patient to the watch. • Encourage patient to look at the watch at repeated intervals and note the time.	Percent of correct responses and types and number of cues required
5. Establish active orientation to place	Scan environment and make a verbal plan to enable patient to move around within the hospital environment.	Percent of self-generated versus clinician-generated cues
	Accompany patient to destination; cue as necessary.	Number of cues required
6. Establish active orientation to time a. Anticipating time intervals	Scan environment or use other temporal aids to enable patient to predict time until a specified event will occur.	Percent of correct predictions
b. Monitoring the passage of time	Indicate when a given time period has elapsed (e.g., ''Tell me when 5 minutes is up'') or estimate amount of time that has elapsed since the beginning of an activity (e.g., ''How long have you been watching this T.V. program?'').	Percent of time variance between actual and patient's estimate
	Estimate time of routine activities; move from simple to complex activities (see Example #4 in Appendix 5–B).	Percent of time variance (see Example #4)
7. Orientation to place—schematic representation	Use maps or floor plans; move from simple diagrams of patient's personal environment to more complicated diagrams of remote environments: • Ask patient to demonstrate route from one place to another. • Answer questions about diagram.	Accuracy of route Percent of correct responses

Perception

Perceptual problems, particularly visual, are a primary characteristic of this population. They require specific therapeutic attention throughout the course of treatment because of their effect on higher cognitive skills.[3] Visuoperceptual tasks will largely center on prereading activities at this point in the treatment hierarchy; however, early orientation activities focus on gross perceptual skills.

In many of the tasks, the clinician may use multiple visual and verbal cues such as red orienting lines on the left and right, guides to focus on a single line, and/or verbal reminders to orient to the left and move eyes to the right.[4,5] The patient should gradually be weaned from reliance on cues. Measurement of the time taken to perform a task may reflect an increase or decrease in response time. This depends on whether the goal is to increase or decrease speed to increase accuracy and monitoring of errors.

Goal	Procedure	Measurement
1. Develop perception of environment	Discriminate environmental noises (e.g., telephone, television, familial voices) with and without background noise.	Percent of correct noises recognized
	See "Attention" and "Orientation" sections.	
2. Develop visuoperceptual skills	Use published prereading materials with designated procedures (see Example #5 in Appendix 5–B) or make similar exercises adapted to needs and interests of the patient.	Percent correct and time required
	Use red line or tactile marker to establish orientation to left side of page. Gradually reduce cues.	Number of orientations to the left within designated time period and number of cues required
	Use computer programs (see Computer Software Bibliography in Appendix 5–C).	Percent correct or score
3. Develop visual scanning and tracking skills	Cancellation tasks (see Example #6 in Appendix 5–B): • Letters: Scan for a given letter varying size of letters, spacing between lines, and number of lines per page. • Words: As above, scan for whole words, all words that begin with a given letter, words by semantic or syntactic category.	Percent correct, time required, and cues required per item
	Scan functional materials for designated information (see Example #7 in Appendix 5–B).	Same as above
	Use computer programs (see Computer Software Bibliography in Appendix 5–C).	Percent correct or score
4. Shift visuoperceptual set	Cancellation tasks. Select a task with at least two variables and alternate between variables (e.g., ask patient to choose items by color; then from the same stimuli, choose items by shape (see Example #8 in Appendix 5–B): • Attributes (color, size, shape). • Letters. • Words.	Percent correct, time required, and cues required to change to a new set

Goal	Procedure	Measurement
5. Improve Writing: a. Spatial organization	Use red and/or raised lines in horizontal and/or vertical positions as a guide for spacing words and sentences (see Example #9 in Appendix 5–B).	Percent of target items spaced correctly within lines
	Use above tasks and gradually eliminate line cues.	Percent of target items spaced correctly and number of cues required
b. Spelling accuracy	Identify perceptually based spelling errors in printed material and patient's own handwriting.	Percent correct and time required
	Correct spelling errors using dictionary for verification as appropriate.	Percent correct
	Fill in missing letters in words (e.g., "b__ok").	Same as above
	Spell to dictation	Same as above
6. Improve Calculation: a. Spatial organization	Follow and maintain columns on calculation tasks using: • A magnetic board. • Lines and boxes (see Example #10 in Appendix 5–B). • Graph paper. • Lined paper. • Unlined paper.	Percent correct and time required
b. Calculation accuracy	Identify calculation errors.	Percent correct identification and time required

Pragmatics

Impairments in pragmatics of communication are now viewed as a major component of the syndrome of right hemisphere damage.[6,3] Disturbances are subtle and include problems with such aspects of communication as prosody and body language, as well as extralinguistic components such as the use of situational context to expedite communication or ability to maintain a topic during dialogue. The clinician will need to consider these communication deficits at all treatment levels. At the attentional level, for example, the clinician will assist the patient in attending to a speaker or shifting attention from speaker to speaker. Orientation to person is often facilitated by awareness of voice suprasegmentals or other idiosyncratic voice characteristics. Awareness of topic often aids memory during a two-way conversation. And, at the highest treatment levels, a patient may need work on discourse organization. In addition to some techniques suggested in this section that are designed to help the patient communicate more effectively, techniques traditionally used for dysarthria and voice problems are applicable for the treatment of prosodic disturbances. Although a few examples are provided below, the reader is directed to voice and dysarthria texts for further examples.[8-10] As in all speech/language training, communication goals should be directed toward receptive and expressive skills as warranted by individual patient needs.

Goal	Procedure	Measurement
1. Improve perception and use prosody/ suprasegmentals:		
a. Stress	Identify or produce different words by syllabic stress patterns (e.g., dessert versus desert).	Percent correct
	Use a dictionary to pronounce words using stress/pronunciation markers.	Same as above
	Use stress patterns to break words into syllables.	Same as above
	Identify or produce different phrases based on stress patterns alone (e.g., All American centers named versus All-American centers named).	Same as above
	Identify or produce rhythmic patterns associated with types of poetry (e.g., limericks).	Same as above
b. Intonation/pause and rate	Identify or use rate, intonation, and pause variation to convey:	Percent correct for identification tasks
	• Different emotional states (e.g., sincere versus sarcastic).	or
	• Different interest or energy levels.	
	• Differences in communicative intent (e.g., request versus inquiry).	Intonation rating on production tasks (see "Behavioral Observation Profile," Appendix 4–B)
	• Turn-taking signals.	
	• Attention-getting signals for new or important information.	
	• Grammatical information or grammatical clarity (e.g., breaking long sentences into phrases).	

Goal	Procedure	Measurement
2. Improve perception of nonvocal cues: a. Eye contact (see section on attention)		
b. Facial expression	Identify negative versus positive emotions as expressed by facial expressions on photographs or in person.	Percent correct
	Interpret facial expressions mimed by the clinician or in photographs (e.g., humorous versus serious; sarcastic versus sincere in photographs).	Percent agreement between clinician and patient
c. Proxemics/body movement and gesture	Choose photograph from an array that depicts a designated attitude (e.g., confident, harried, angry, relaxed).	Percent correct
3. Improve pragmatic skills (contextual determinants)	Teach patient the following pragmatic strategies for use of situational context/cues:	Pretest; post-test over time

	• Ellipsis—delete information understood from context.
	  • Social constraints—vary communication style in different types of social situations (e.g., direct versus indirect requests; see Example #11 in Appendix 5–B).
	  • Deixis—use terms that change relative to speaker versus listener (e.g., come–go; this–that; you–me; here–there).	

	Practice identifying violations in the use of linguistic contextual cues:	Percent agreement between clinician and patient

	• Note topic digression in written transcripts or audio tapes of patient's own dialogues.
	  • Identify communication inadequacies or ambiguities in written transcripts or audio tapes of patient's own dialogue.
	  • Note inappropriately referenced pronouns (e.g., ''I talked to him'' in which referent for him is not clearly specified).	

	Teach patient the following discourse cohesion devices for use of linguistic contextual cues:	Pretest; post-test over time

	• Feedback (e.g., ''I understand.'' or ''Do you mean . . . ?'')
	  • Cataphoric reference (e.g., ''We will be covering three topics.'')
	  • Anaphoric reference (e.g., ''as stated before . . .'')
	  • Contingent queries (e.g., ''who do you mean by 'he'?'')	

Goal	Procedure	Measurement
	Teach patient strategies for use of knowledge about other participants in a conversation (e.g., shared knowledge—you do not have to tell your mother where you were born).	Same as above
	Practice dialogue skills:	Same as above
	• Turn-taking (e.g., turn-taking in card and board games, conversation)	
	• Interviewing techniques—have patient ask questions to learn about your job and interests.	
	• Information gathering—use ''twenty questions'' strategy to organize questioning skills.	

Memory

Memory problems are another persisting characteristic of patients with right hemisphere damage, especially retention of visually coded information.[11,12] Treatment will focus on developing conscious awareness of the need to use strategies, identifying strategies useful to the patient, and facilitating use of these strategies. It is our experience that memory is one of the most difficult areas to train through treatment. Success will require counseling of family members to use techniques at home and organize the environment to facilitate retention.[13]

Memory is not a unitary phenomenon. It is affected by variables such as attention,[1,2] distractibility, poor encoding, time restraints, perseverative or rigid behavior, and impulsivity.[14] Memory is an active process and requires conscious and deliberate use of strategies.[15] See Example 12, Appendix 5–B, for a list of strategies. One can therapeutically separate memory processes into facilitation (building associations, out-of-place images, mnemonics, rehearsal, saliency, chunking) or compensation (lists, calendars, tapes, card catalogues, organizing environment). The focus of this section will be on developing these functional strategies rather than on improving storage capacity.

Goal	*Procedure*	*Measurement*
1. Develop facilitory and compensatory strategies	Use question/answer format to teach patient to use a memory book for retrieval of general information (see Example #13 in Appendix 5–B): • Demographic. • Daily schedule. • Significant people. • Personal events, experience. • Factual information (e.g., current events, reading material).	Accuracy of using memory book within designated time period with gradual withdrawal of cues
	Use memory book during a conversation for retrieval of above information.	Percent correct
	Teach patient rehearsal and association strategies for remembering names (see Example #12 in Appendix 5–B): • Use photographs of family members, famous persons, persons known to the patient, hospital personnel, and professional associates. • Practice rehearsal of names in meaningful contexts (see Example #12 in Appendix 5–B) or use in meaningful sentences (e.g., ''Mary is my wife''). • See section on Orientation to Person.	Accuracy of recall within designated time period with gradual withdrawal of cues
2. Generalize facilitory and compensatory strategies	Practice use of a specific strategy during a treatment session; then have patient apply the same strategy in a different setting, at a different time, and/or with new people.	Accuracy of recall within designated time period with gradual withdrawal of cues
3. Develop retention of written material	Apply above strategies (see Example #12 in Appendix 5–B) for remembering written material geared toward needs and interests of patient; control for length, complexity, vocabulary, and print size.	Number of correct responses and time required (as appropriate)
4. Develop compensatory skills for residual memory limitations	Counsel family, patient, and/or staff on ways to organize environment and daily activities to aid memory.	Family and staff feedback

Integration

Integration is one of the primary functions of the right hemisphere. We believe that integration disturbances contribute to the visual perception, attention, and memory problems exhibited by these patients. At higher processing levels, integration disturbances are seen in tasks requiring verbal and nonverbal problem solving, hypothesis testing, drawing inferences, making predictions, and interpretive thinking. In this section, several types of integrative tasks appropriate for the mildly involved right hemisphere-damaged patients are presented. These tasks would be applicable to any cortically damaged individual depending on educational level, premorbid problem-solving skill, and interest level.

Goal	Procedure	Measurement
1. Improve judgment and problem-solving skills.	Identify inconsistencies: • In pictures (e.g., a shoe instead of a glove on a hand) • Verbal absurdities	Percent correct
	Anticipate responses to problem situations (e.g., fires, traffic jams, personal hazards).	Percent of agreement between clinician and patient
	Formulate alternate solutions to a single problem.	Same as above
	Plan how to carry out everyday tasks (e.g., writing a letter, paying a bill, planning a party); use verbal and/or written notes as necessary.	Same as above
	Role-play functional situations with clinician and in groups.	Same as above
	Use computer programs (see Computer Software Bibliography in Appendix 5–C).	Percent correct or score
2. Improve organizational skills:		
a. Sequencing	Sequence the following: • Letters of the alphabet. • Letters into words. • Words alphabetically. • Words into sentences. • Sentences into paragraphs. • Paragraphs into short stories. • Daily or familiar activities. • Less familiar activities (e.g., trip itinerary, things-to-do list, moving, income tax).	Percent correct
b. Prioritizing	Prioritize specific items within: • Activities of daily living. • A shopping list. • A things-to-do list. • Less familiar activities (e.g., moving to a new residence). • A budget.	Percent of details prioritized

Goal	*Procedure*	*Measurement*
c. Outlining	Take notes from visual or auditory material; gradually increase complexity of stimulus.	Percent of pertinent facts included and/or percent correctly ordered
	Outline to prepare for speeches, memos, letters, and so on.	Same as above
	Outline by topic or category.	Same as above
3. Improve abstract reasoning skills	Recognize fallacies in reasoning tasks.	Percent correct and time required
	Practice inductive reasoning tasks:	Percent correct and time required
	• Determining relevancy.	
	• Determining cause and effect relationships.	
	• Reasoning by analogy.	
	• Drawing conclusions.	
	• Drawing morals from a story.	
	Practice deductive reasoning tasks (e.g., syllogisms).	Percent correct
	Perceiving relationships:	Percent correct
	Familial relationships (e.g., "Who is Mary's uncle if Mary is my mother?").	
	• Part–whole relationships.	
	• Similarities and differences.	
	• Categorizing.	
	Practice imagery tasks:	Percent correct
	• Interpret visual symbolic materials (e.g., cartoons).	
	• Interpret visual representation of metaphors, similes, and idioms.	
	• Interpret auditory representation of similes and so on.	
	Interpret and appreciate humor:	Percent correct
	• Puns and double meanings.	
	• Cartoons and political satire.	
	• Humorists (e.g., Andy Rooney, Erma Bombeck).	
	• Anecdotes (e.g., Thurber fables).	

REFERENCES

1. Strub RL, Black FW: *The Mental Status Examination in Neurology*. Philadelphia, FA Davis, 1977.

2. Strub RL, Black FW: *Organic Brain Syndromes: An Introduction to Neurobehavioral Disorders*. Philadelphia, FA Davis, 1981.

3. Myers PS: Right hemisphere impairment, in Holland AL (ed): *Language Disorders in Adults*. San Diego, College-Hill Press, 1984, pp 177–208.

4. Diller L, Gordon MA, Gerstmann LJ, et al: Training sensory awareness and spatial organization in people with right brain damage. *Arch Phys Med Rehabil* 1979;60:491–496.

5. Stanton KM, Yorkston KM, Kenyon VT, et al: Language utilization in teaching reading to left neglect patients, in Brookshire RH (ed): *Clinical Aphasiology: Proceedings of the Conference*. Minneapolis, BRK Publishers, 1981, pp 262–271.

6. Lemon P, Burns M, Lehner L: Communication deficits associated with right cerebral brain damage. Presented at the American-Speech-Language-Hearing Association Convention, Atlanta, 1979.

7. Myers PS: Right hemisphere impairment, in Holland AL (ed): *Language Disorders in Adults*. San Diego, College-Hill Press, 1984, pp 177–208.

8. Fairbanks G: *Voice and Articulation Drillbook*. New York, Harper & Brothers, 1960.

9. Boone DR: *The Voice and Voice Therapy*. Englewood Cliffs, NJ, Prentice-Hall, 1971.

10. Fisher HB: *Improving Voice and Articulation*, 2nd ed. Boston, Houghton-Mifflin, 1975.

11. Riege WH, Metter EJ, Hanson WR: Verbal and non-verbal recognition memory in aphasic and nonaphasic stroke patients. *Brain Lang* 1980;10:60–70.

12. Whitehouse PJ: Imagery and verbal encoding in left and right hemisphere damaged patients. *Brain Lang* 1981;14:315–332.

13. Burns M: A treatment approach for recency memory deficit of neurological origin. *J Illinois Speech Hear Assoc* 1979;12:1–5.

14. Burns M, Halper A, Mogil S: *Communication Problems in Right Hemispheric Brain Damage: Diagnostic and Treatment Approaches*. Chicago, Rehabilitation Institute of Chicago, 1983.

15. Menyuk P, Menn L: Early strategies for the perception and production of words and sounds, in Fletcher P, Garman M (eds): *Language Acquisition: Studies in First Language Development*. Cambridge, Cambridge University Press, 1979.

Appendix 5–A

Guidelines for Communication Management:
Family and Staff

REHABILITATION INSTITUTE OF CHICAGO

- Treat the individual as an adult.

- Strive for communication, not perfection.

- Provide reassurance and redirect attention to another task or topic when the individual swears, cries, or displays emotional outbursts.

- Routinize daily schedule.

- Organize the home environment to aid memory.

- Structure and minimize auditory and visual stimulation to permit better attention to the task at hand.

- Rearrange the environment to use right visual field.

- Compensate for visual impairments through verbal mediation.

- Supplement all directions with simple repeated verbal cues, if necessary.

- Draw attention to visual reference points in the room, such as doorways and furniture (e.g., paint the doorknob a bright color or post a large label).

- Avoid rapid movements around the individual.

- Establish attention prior to giving a message to the individual.

- Repeat a statement when uncertain whether the individual was attending.

- Be aware that individual's lack of affect does not necessarily signal disinterest or depression.

- Ask questions during a conversation to ensure that the individual remembers and follows topic changes.

- Encourage the individual to plan out a task by breaking up the task into a specified number of small steps.

- Decrease impulsivity by encouraging the individual to slow down.

Source: Adapted from Halper AS, Glista S: Language and speech disorders of neurological origin in adults, in Martin N, Holt N, and Hicks B (eds): *Comprehensive Rehabilitation Nursing*. New York, McGraw Hill, 1981, and Halper AS, Mogil S: The role of the speech language pathologist and audiologist, in Olson D, Granger C (eds): *Rehabilitating the Aged Disabled*. Woburn, MA, Butterworth, in press.

Appendix 5–B

Examples of Treatment Tasks

EXAMPLE #1: ATTENTIONAL TASKS

Level: Attention
Goal: Shifting attentional set
Measurement: Percent of appropriate shifts and length of time required to change attentional set

Procedure #1—Vary Input Modes:

A.   Visual input only:
    Instruction: "Point to the dots that match the color of the dot on the left."

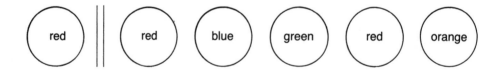

B.   Auditory and visual input:
    Instruction: "Listen to me. I will name a color. You point to all dots of the color I say, . . . red."

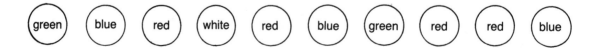

C.   Auditory input only:
    Instruction: "Every time I say the color blue, tap your finger, . . . green . . .red . . . blue . . . orange."

Procedure #2—Vary Stimulus Materials:

Instruction: ''Point to the letters that match the letter on the left.''

A ‖ CDNABLACHAKBSRATMORALB

Instruction: ''Point to the dots that match the size of the dot on the left. . . . Now point to the dots that match the color of the dot on the left.''

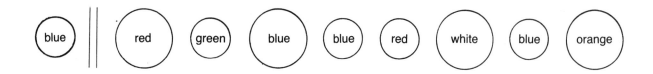

Procedure #3—Vary Response Requirements:

Instruction: ''Underline the letters that match the letter on the left.''

L ‖ RTLMOLRPKILRCKLTOLC

Instruction: ''Circle the letters that match the letter on the left.''

L ‖ RTLMOLRPKILRCKLTOLC

Note: Gradually increase complexity of tasks by increasing number of stimuli, decreasing size, and combining any of the above subgoals.

EXAMPLE #2: SAMPLE CORE ORIENTATION ITEMS

Level: Orientation
Goal: Establish knowledge of basic biographical/environmental information
Measurement: Number of stimulus repetitions required to obtain accurate response or percent of correct facts provided

> Patient name
>
> Day
>
> Date
>
> Present location
>
> Home address
>
> Home phone number
>
> Significant family members' names and pertinent data (e.g., married/single, number of children, number of grandchildren)
>
> Time of day
>
> Reason for hospitalization

EXAMPLE #3: RECOGNITION OF PERSONS

Level: Orientation
Goal: Establish orientation to person
Measurement: Percent of correct responses

Procedure: Present simultaneously photographs and brief audio recordings (if possible). Have patient name; use the following cues as necessary.

> Male/female
> Adult/child
> Old/young
> Hair color
> Body size
> Distinguishing facial features (e.g., scar, large nose, beard, unusual eye color), unusual voice characteristics (e.g., habitual use of O.K., accent)

EXAMPLE #4: ESTIMATING TIME OF ROUTINE AND COMPLETE ACTIVITIES

(Clinician assists patient in identifying details and estimating time)

Level: Orientation
Goal: Establish active orientation to time
Measurement: Percent of time variance

Activity: Time

1.   Concrete or Routine (getting ready in the morning)   Patient's Original Estimate: <u>10 minutes</u>

      Assist patient to estimate time intervals:

      a. Get out of bed and turn off alarm   <u>2</u>
      b. Brush teeth   <u>5</u>
      c. Shower   <u>15</u>
      d. Put on makeup or shave   <u>10</u>
      e. Get dressed   <u>10</u>
      f. Eat breakfast   <u>20</u>

      Total estimated time with assistance   <u>62</u>

      Percent of time variance

$$\frac{\text{Assisted (62)} - \text{estimated (10)} = 52}{\text{Estimated with assistance} = 62} =$$ <u>84%</u>

2.   Complex (Christmas shopping scenario)   Patient's Original Estimate: <u>   </u>

      a. Make a list of persons   <u>   </u>
         (e.g., 2 children, 4 grandchildren, 1 spouse, 2 in-laws, 6 friends)
      b. Decide on presents and cost   <u>   </u>
      c. Decide on stores   <u>   </u>
      d. Buy presents   <u>   </u>
         (e.g., considering travel time, change in list, waiting in lines, trying a different store,
         out-of-stock items)
      Total estimated time with assistance   <u>   </u>
      Percent of time variance   <u>   </u>

PLE #5: PREREADING MATERIALS

Level: Perception
Goal: Develop visuoperceptual skills
Measurement: Percent correct and time required

	VM	VC	VD	SR	FG	FC	VMI
Fitzhugh[1]							
101 Shape matching			x		x	x	
102 Shape completion	x	x					
103 Shape analysis and sequencing	x			x	x		
Frostig[2]							
Figure–ground			x		x		x
Constancy of shape				x	x	x	
Position in space				x	x		
Spatial relationships				x	x		x
DLM[3]							
Colored inch cubes	x		x	x	x		
Colored inch cube designs	x		x	x	x		
Colored inch cube designs in perspective	x		x	x	x		
Large parquetry blocks	x		x	x	x		
Large parquetry designs	x		x	x	x		
Small parquetry designs I, II, III	x		x	x	x		
Small parquetry blocks	x		x	x	x		
Multivariant sequencing beads	x		x	x	x		
Multivariant sequencing bead patterns	x		x	x	x		
Eye–hand integration exercises I							x
Eye–hand integration exercises II		x					x
Visual discrimination flip books I, II, III			x	x			
Visual sequential memory exercises	x		x	x			
Visual memory cards: I colors, II objects, III shapes, IV patterns	x		x	x			
Same or different design cards	x		x	x			
Visual matching memory and sequencing exercises, book 1–6	x		x	x			

Legend: VM, visual memory; VC, visual closure; VD, visual discrimination; SR, spatial relationships; FG, figure–ground; FC, form constancy; VMI, visuomotor integration.

---

1. The Fitzhugh Plus Program: Allied Educational Press, P.O. Box 337, Niles, Michigan 49120.
2. The Developmental Program in Visual Perception by Marianne Frostig, Follett Publishing Company, Chicago, Illinois 60607.
3. DLM Teaching Resources, One DLM Park, Allen, Texas 75002.

EXAMPLE #6: TYPES OF CANCELLATION TASKS

Level: Perception
Goal: Develop visual scanning and tracking skills
Measurement: Percent correct, time required, and cues required per item

Instructions: Scan for the letter on the left

B   L   B   M   K   T   B   M   C   E   B   D   E   R   L   P

F   F   G   H   M   T   K   L   P   R   F   B   E   E   F   B   L   Y   E   F   B   F   P

c   ckldmbckstmcmetopupdcvmtmuoldcvgodcbemciroc

Instructions: Scan for the word that matches the word on the left

PULL   PUSH PULL LUMP COOL BULL PULL FULL PULL

Instructions: Scan for all words that begin with *SH*

SHOOT SHY WISH SHARE SHIP LOOP HOOT PUSH

Instructions: Scan for all the color words

RED BIG BLUE YELLOW SAME SHIP ONE GREEN TWO GREY SMOKE

Instructions: Scan for all prepositions

ON IN OUT FULL OVER UNDER IN UP STAY WITH DOWN OUT BYE

EXAMPLE #7: FUNCTIONAL MATERIALS FOR SCANNING AND TRACKING

Level: Perception
Goal: Develop visual scanning and tracking skills
Measurement: Percent correct, time required, and cues required per item

Procedure: Scan for designated information (e.g., phone number of John Jones; TV programs Tuesday at 9:00 PM)

Bus schedules
Dictionary
Directions on food packages
Grocery lists
Local magazine listings of activities (e.g., movies, restaurants, night clubs)
Menu
Newspaper ads
Newspaper headlines
Phone book
Racing form
Recipes
Table of contents
TV guide
Vending machines

EXAMPLE #8: SAMPLE TASKS FOR SHIFTING VISUOPERCEPTUAL SET

Level: Perception
Goal: Shift visuoperceptual set
Measurement: Percent correct, time required, and cues required to change to a new set

---

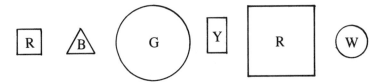

Set 1—Patient identifies all squares

Set 2—Patient identifies all red shapes

Set 3—Patient identifies all large shapes

ALCqErFnMRoSyzPmqLtdNZe

Set 1—Patient identifies all upper case letters

Set 2—Patient identifies all lower case letters

Set 3—Patient identifies all vowels

Set 4—Patient identifies all consonants

---

cat   show   red   nice   dog   nine   jacket   yellow

Set 1—Patient identifies all animals (category)

Set 2—Patient identifies all words that end in ''e''

Set 3—Patient identifies all two-syllable words

EXAMPLE #9: SPATIAL AID FOR WRITING

Level: Perception
Goal: Improve writing: spatial organization
Measurement: Percent of target items spaced correctly within lines

EXAMPLE #10: FOLLOWING AND MAINTAINING COLUMNS FOR CALCULATION

Level: Perception
Goal: Improve calculation: spatial organization
Measurement: Percent correct and time required

```
  3 8 7                  7 8 1
    2 6                    3 4
  5 9 3                  6 9 5
  2 8 7                  2 8 7
  ☐☐☐☐
```

```
                         7 8 9
                    ×      6 5
                         ☐☐☐☐
                         ☐☐☐☐
                        ☐☐☐☐☐
```

```
        ☐☐
    7 / 5 3 9
```

EXAMPLE #11: SAMPLES OF DIRECT VERSUS INDIRECT REQUESTS

Level: Nonverbal communication
Goal: Improve pragmatic skills
Measurement: Pretest; post-test over time

Direct Requests:

a.   May I use your phone?

b.   Please hand me that book.

c.   Please tell me the time.

d.   Please look at the page.

e.   Give me a better answer.

Indirect Requests:

a.   Do you have a phone here?

b.   Could you hand me that book?

c.   Do you have the time?

d.   Are you looking at the page?

e.   Is that the best answer?

Other examples of indirect requests:

a.   Are you ready to get started?

(Patient should prepare to work, not answer question.)

b.   There's the bell.

(Patient should get ready to stop working, not look for a bell.)

c.   That's the left side of the page?

(Patient should attempt to correct error, not answer question.)

d.   Why don't you look at me?

(Patient should establish eye contact, not respond to question.)

e.   Have you heard the joke about the ____ ?

(Patient should signal you to tell the joke by saying "no," not ask questions about it.)

EXAMPLE #12: STRATEGIES FOR MEMORY*

I. Facilitation Strategies

  A. Rehearsal

  When first introduced to a new person, ask the person to spell or pronounce his name clearly and distinctly; repeat this several times during your initial conversation.

> Mary: "Hi! My name is Mary Peters."
> Patient: "Hi, Mary! My name is John. Mary, how do you spell Peters?"

  B. Saliency

  Focus on the most important information within a message and then the least meaningful information. When taking a telephone message, note the name, telephone number, and so on, first; then complete the contextual information. When taking notes in a class, write dates and names before writing other contentive information.

  C. Chunking

  Create meaningful groups for details.

> Phone number 864-3642 recalled as "eight, sixty-four, thirty-six, forty-two."

  D. Mnemonics

  Acronyms—formulate a word from the first letter of items.

> Susan the Speech Pathologist = *SOS* = Susan of Speech.
> To get hospital operator = *DOO* = Dial 0 for Operator.

  Rhyme and melody—formulate a rhyme to link words.

> Thirty days hath September, April, June, and November.
> Wheelchair mobility—a heel and a toe and away we go.

  E. Visual Imagery (Patients may vary in their ability to benefit from static versus action images.)

  Conventional images—associate and relate interacting pairs of items:

> Mary Brown is married and has brown hair.
> The supermarket "Jewel" versus a gemstone.

  Absurd images—Make a novel or ridiculous connection with an item.

> Mary Burns with her hair on fire.
> Mr. Lee with a Sara Lee pie on his face.

  Exaggerated images—Create an image of an item in exaggerated form.

> Speech pathologist with a loud voice.
> The doctor using six stethoscopes.

---

*Adapted from Lorayne H, Lucas J: *The Memory Book*. New York, Stein & Day, 1974, and Zachmeister, EB, Nyberg, SE. *Human Memory: An Introduction to Research & Theory*. Monterey, California: Brooks/Cole Publishing Company, 1982.

Out-of-proportion images—Visualize an aspect of an item as larger or smaller than natural.

The physical therapist associated with a large cane.
The audiologist with huge ears.

Out-of-place images—Visualize an item in an unexpected place.

To remember keys, place them next to the coffee pot.
To remember to complete homework, tape it over the television screen.
To remember to practice range-of-motion exercises, place sling on top of television.

II. Compensation Strategies

A. Keep lists.

Make shopping lists, things-to-do lists.

B. Use calendar and memory books.

Include daily schedules, names of important persons and places, and questions frequently asked by the patient or of the patient and his or her answers (see also Example #13).

C. Use Dictaphone or tape recorder for daily reminders.

D. Create card file and catalogues of names as appropriate.

Cross-classify associates alphabetically and by professional association.

E. Organize home environment: have a designated place for all routinely used items.

Reorganize closets to avoid repetition of clothes within a few days.

EXAMPLE #13: SAMPLE MEMORY BOOK INCLUSIONS

Level: Memory
Goal: Develop facilitory and compensatory strategies
Measurement: Accuracy of using memory book within a designated time period with gradual withdrawal of cues

Demographic Information:

Name

Addresss

Phone number

Birthday

Occupation

Spouse

Children

Age

Reason for hospitalization

Daily Schedule:

Close Relatives:

Aunts

Uncles

In-laws

Grandchildren

Important Names:

Work

Hospital staff

Special friends

Personal Events and Experiences:

Special trips

Evening and weekend activities

Factual Information:

President

Vice president

Mayor

Other Important Information Frequently Used:

Phone numbers

Addresses

Birthdays

Appendix 5–C

Annotated Bibliography of Diagnostic and Treatment Materials

COMMERCIALLY AVAILABLE MATERIALS

Key

Population

Lo (Low)—Severe and moderately severe (see diagnostic section for description, Appendix 4–B).

Hi (High)—Moderate, mild, and minimal (see diagnostic section for description, Appendix 4–B).

Processing Level

O—Orientation
P—Perception
Pr—Pragmatics
M—Memory
JPS—Judgment and problem-solving skills
Org—Organizational skills
AR—Abstract reasoning
*—Adaptable for use within designated area.

	Population		Processing Level						
	Lo	Hi	O	P	Pr	M	JPS	Org	AR
A Diversity of Puzzles by E. R. Emmet. Barnes and Noble Books, 10 East 53rd St., New York, NY 10022. Includes puzzles of increasing difficulty designed to improve abstract ability and everyday problem-solving tasks.		x		x		x			
Basic Thinking Skills by Anita Harnadek. Midwest Publication Co., P.O. Box 448, Pacific Grove, CA 93950.									
"Analogies: A–D" Contains exercises on interpretation and use of analogies		x							x
"Antonyms and Synonyms" Contains three sets of exercises for antonyms and synonyms		x							x
"Antonyms, Synonyms, Similarities and Differences" Contains exercises covering antonyms, synonyms, similarities, and differences		x							x
"Following Directions A–B" Paper and pencil activities for following increasingly complex directions		x		x		x			
"Miscellaneous, Including Transitivity and Same Person or Not?" Contains activities for relationships and drawing conclusions		x							x
"Patterns" Contains activities for analysis and synthesis of visual patterns		x		x					x
"Think About It" Contains activities for problem solving requiring deduction and inferences		x					x		x
"What Would You Do? and True to Life, or Fantasy?" Contains activities for solving hypothetical everyday problems		x					x		x
Building Thinking Skills I & II by Howard Black and Sandra Black. Midwest Publication Co., P.O. Box 448, Pacific Grove, CA 93950. A variety of thinking exercises organized into similarities and differences, sequences, classification, and analogy		x	x	x			x	x	x
Cognitive Reorganization: A Stimulus Handbook by Sharon M. Halloran and Elizabeth J. Bressler. C.C. Publications, Inc., P.O. Box 23699, Tigard, OR 97223-0108. Contains exercises and functional activities for orientation and memory, word association, problem solving, and abstract reasoning	x	x	x			x	x	x	x
Creative Growth Games Jove Publications, 757 Third Ave., New York, NY 10017. Contains numerical, verbal, and spatial games designed to increase everyday problem-solving activities		x		x					x
Critical Thinking Book I & II by Anita Harnadek. Midwest Publication Co., P.O. Box 448, Pacific Grove, CA 93950. Designed to incorporate group discussion with specific problems to sharpen thinking skills		x					x	x	x

	Population		Processing Level						
	Lo	Hi	O	P	Pr	M	JPS	Org	AR
Everyday Reading and Writing by Frank Laubach, Elizabeth Kirk, and Robert Laubach. New Readers Press, Box 131, Syracuse, NY 13210. Includes work in reading signs, labels, maps, instructions, reference books, newspapers, magazines, and so on and in writing business and personal letters	x	x				x	x	x	
Fill in the Blanks by Stephen D. Match. Mafex Associates, Inc., 90 Cherry St., Box 519, Johnstown, PA 15907. Contains samples of forms and functional activities such as keeping a checkbook	x	x	x					x	
Gates-Peardon Reading Exercises by Arthur I. Gates and Celeste C. Peardon. Teachers College Press, c/o Harper & Row, Keystone Industrial Park, Scranton, PA 18512. Contains short story material followed by questions on main idea, remembering details, and following directions		x				x			*
Graduate Record Examination: Aptitude Tests by David R. Turner. Arco, 219 Park Avenue South, New York, NY 10003. Includes activities for reading comprehension, mathematics, vocabulary, and so on		x				x	x		x
High School Equivalency Test (GED) General Review for the Exam by Gary R. Gruber. Monarch Press, 1230 Avenue of the Americas, New York, NY 10020. Includes sample tests and drills in grammar, spelling, writing style, reading comprehension and interpretation, vocabulary, and mathematics		x				x	x		x
Inductive Thinking Skills by Anita Harnadek. Midwest Publication Co., P.O. Box 448, Pacific Grove, CA 93950.									
"Cause and Effect" Contains problems designed to differentiate between events that have a cause and effect relationship and those that are simultaneous, sequential, coincidental, or somehow related		x							x
"Figure Patterns" Contains activities for determining figure relationships and figure patterns		x		x					x
"Inferences: A and B" Contains activities for determining reasonable and unreasonable inferences for real-life situations		x					x		x
"Open Ended Problems" Contains activities designed to stimulate analysis, reflection, and synthesis of knowledge from various experiences		x					x		x
"Reasoning by Analogy" Contains activities for application of analogies to real-life situations		x					x		x

	Population		Processing Level						
	Lo	Hi	O	P	Pr	M	JPS	Org	AR
"Relevant Information" Contains activities for determining relevancy of a statement to a given problem		x							x
McCall-Crabbs Standard Test Lessons in Reading by William A. McCall and Lelah Mae Crabbs. Teachers College Press, c/o Harper & Row, Keystone Industrial Park, Scranton, PA 18512. Contains increasingly complex, short prose paragraphs of general interest; a multiple-choice quiz follows each selection		x				x			*
McCall-Crabbs Standard Test Lessons in Reading by William A. McCall and Edwin H. Smith. Teachers College Press, c/o Harper & Row, Keystone Industrial Park, Scranton, PA 18512. Includes lessons for improving ability to reason clearly and read critically at high school and college levels		x							x
Manual of Exercises for Expressive Reasoning (MEER) by Linda Zachman, Carol Jorgensen, Mark Barrett, Rosemary Huisingh, and Mary Kay Snedden. LinguiSystems, Inc., 1630 Fifth Ave., Suite 806, Moline, IL 61265. Contains exercises for thought formulation, organization, and expression		x					x	x	x
Mind Benders (Deductive Thinking Skills) A1–A3, B1–B4, C1–C3 by Anita Harnadek. Midwest Publication Co., P.O. Box 448, Pacific Grove, CA 93950. Contains exercises to develop deductive reasoning skills		x				*	x		x
Motts Basic Language Skill Programs: Series 600 and 900. Allied Educational Press, P.O. Box 737, Niles, MI 49120. Includes drills on survival skills, various language skills, spelling, and reading	x	x			x				
New Reading – Thinking Skills by Ethel S. Maney and Anne F. Kroehler. The Continental Press, Inc., P.O. Box 554, Elgin, Il 60120 or Elizabethtown, PA 17022. Contains drills on word meaning, evaluating and organizing ideas, problem solving, making inferences, generalization and judgments, and determining relationships		x				x	x	x	x
News For You: A and B. New Readers Press, Box 131, Syracuse, NY 13210. Contains captioned pictures, headlines, and articles ranging from two to three related sentences up to approximately six paragraphs in a large print weekly newspaper at a fourth to sixth grade reading level		x		x		*	*	*	*
Occupations Caroline Blakely, ed. New Readers Press, Box 131, Syracuse, NY 13210. Includes job descriptions and short features on people in various occupations such as service occupations, para-professionals, and government services		x				x	*	*	x

	Population		Processing Level						
	Lo	Hi	O	P	Pr	M	JPS	Org	AR

Practice in Survival Reading: Books 2–8 New Readers Press, Box 131, Syracuse, NY 13210.
Includes reading instructions, newspapers, maps and labels for reading level grades 3–6; interest level renders material adaptive for adult life styles

	Lo	Hi	O	P	Pr	M	JPS	Org	AR
Book 2—"Signs Around Town" by Calvin Greatsinger	x		x		x		x	*	
Book 3—"Label Talk" by Calvin Greatsinger	x		x		x		x	*	
Book 4—"Read the Instructions First" by Calvin Greatsinger	x		x		x		x	*	
Book 5—"Your Daily Paper" by Wendy Stein	x		x		x		x	x	
Book 6—"It's On the Map" by Patricia Waelder			x	x	x			x	
Book 7—"Let's Look It Up" by Patricia Waelder			x		x		x		
Book 8—"Caution: Fine Print Ahead" by Patricia Waelder			x		x		x		x

Reader's Digest Reading Skill Builders and Advanced Reading Skill Builders and accompanying *Audio Lessons.* Reader's Digest Services, Inc., Educational Division, Pleasantville, NY 10570.
Contains story material at varying reading grade levels; exercises, quizzes, and discussion questions follow each story

	Lo	Hi	O	P	Pr	M	JPS	Org	AR
			x				x		x

Reading and Thinking (Exercises for Developing Reading Comprehension and Critical Thinking Skills) by A. J. Evans.
Teachers College Press, c/o Harper & Row, Keystone Industrial Park, Scranton, PA 18512.
Contains stories designed to foster critical thinking

	Lo	Hi	O	P	Pr	M	JPS	Org	AR
			x				x	x	x

Recovery from Right Hemisphere Brain Damage by Kathleen Anderson and Pamela Crowe Miller.
C. C. Publications, Inc., P.O. Box 23699, Tigard, OR 97223-0108.

	Lo	Hi	O	P	Pr	M	JPS	Org	AR
"Memory" Contains exercises for recall of daily activities, years, shapes, and so on.	x		x	x	x		x	x	x
"Reading and Writing" Contains functional reading and writing activities.	x		x		x				
"Self-Perception" Contains exercises for development of body concept, personal attitudes, and so on.	x		x	x	x	x	x	x	x
"Thought Organization" Contains verbal and nonverbal activities for sequencing, patterning, mathematical problem solving, and so on.	x		x	x	x			x	x
"Visual Perception and Attention" Contains exercises for visual discrimination, clock imagery, maps, and so on.	x		x	x	x				

Study Type of Reading Exercises: Secondary School Level and College Level by Ruth Strang.
Teachers College Press, c/o Harper & Row, Keystone Industrial Park, Scranton, PA 18512.
Includes articles of increasing length on reading, study methods, and efficiency.

	Lo	Hi	O	P	Pr	M	JPS	Org	AR
			x				x	x	x

	Population		Processing Level						
	Lo	Hi	O	P	Pr	M	JPS	Org	AR
Supermarket by Fern Tripp. Fern Tripp, 2035 E. Sierra Way, Dinuba, CA 93618. Contains problems in grocery buying, making change, check writing, and so on.		x	x			x	x	*	
Syllogisms A1–C1 (Deductive Reasoning Activities) by Michael O. Baker. Midwest Publication Co., P.O. Box 448, Pacific Grove, CA 93950. Contains exercises for deductive reasoning to strengthen analytical thinking.		x							x
Test Lessons in Figurative Language by William A. McCall, Edwin H. Smith, and Barbara C. Palmer. Teachers College Press c/o Harper & Row, Keystone Industrial Park, Scranton, PA 18512. Contains high level lessons on use and interpretation of figurative language.		x							x
Twenty Words a Day to Perfect Spelling by Claude W. Faulkner. Visual Education Association, 321 Hopeland St., Dayton, OH 45208. Includes 1,000 study cards giving spelling and definition of words most commonly misspelled by high school students.		x	x						
Using the Newspaper by Larry Parsky. Mafex Associates, Inc., 90 Cherry St., Box 519, Johnstown, PA 15907. Contains exercises for practice with newspaper scanning and reading.		x	x						
Using the Telephone by Cheri Cook. New Readers Press, Box 131, Syracuse, NY 13210. Contains exercises for common telephone usage, including using the telephone directory, telephone courtesy, and using a business telephone.		x	x			x	x		
Verbal Classifications by Howard Black and Sandra Black. Midwest Publication Co., P.O. Box 448, Pacific Grove, CA 93950. Contains exercises for verbal classification.		x						x	x
Verbal Sequences A1–C1 by Howard Black and Sandra Black. Midwest Publication Co., P.O. Box 448, Pacific Grove, CA 93950. Contains exercises for verbal sequencing and prioritizing.		x					x	x	x
Visual Logic by Jerzy T. Cwirko-Godycki and Janina E. Karczmarczyk. Midwest Publication Co., P.O. Box 448, Pacific Grove, CA 93950. Contains deductive reasoning with pictorial and graphic stimuli.									
"Conjunction Visual Logic"				x		x			x
"Disjunction Visual Logic"				x		x			x
"Negation Visual Logic"				x		x			x
"Three Connectives Visual Logic."				x		x			x
Vocabulary Building Exercises for the Young Adult by Dorothy McCarr. Dormac, Inc., P.O. Box 1699, Beaverton, OR 97075-1699. Contains exercises for dictionary use, alphabetizing, and word games.		x	x					x	

	Population		Processing Level						
	Lo	Hi	O	P	Pr	M	JPS	Org	AR
Wordly Wise 1–9 by Kenneth Hodkinson and Joseph Ornato. Educators Publishing Service, Inc., 75 Moulton St., Cambridge, MA 02238-6706. Contains crossword puzzles, analogies, and so on.		x		x					x
Workbook for Aphasia: Exercises for the Redevelopment of Higher Language Functioning by Susan Howell Brubaker. Wayne State University Press, Detroit, MI 48202. Contains exercises for sequencing, following directions, improving concrete and abstract reasoning, and so on.	x	x					x	x	x
Workbook for Reasoning Skills: Exercises for Cognitive Facilitation by Susan Howell Brubaker. Wayne State University Press, Detroit, MI 48202. Contains exercises to develop skills in drawing conclusions, problem solving, following directions, sequencing, humor, and so on.	x	x		x			x	x	x

SELECTED COMPUTER SOFTWARE PUBLISHERS AND CATALOGUES

The following is a list of some companies and catalogues that offer computer software applicable to treatment of patients with right hemisphere damage. An exhaustive list of all software would be impossible because of continual changes in programs and additions to catalogues. It is recommended that the clinician review available software prior to purchasing.*

Beckley-Cardy Company
  Corporate Office
  7500 Old Oak Boulevard
  Cleveland, OH 44130

Compu-tations, Inc.
  P.O. Box 502
  Troy, MI 48099

Developmental Learning Materials
  One DLM Park
  Allen, TX 75002

Edu-ware Services, Inc.
  22222 Sherman Way
  Canoga Park, CA 91303

Hartley Courseware, Inc.
  123 Bridge Street
  Box 419
  Dimondale, MI 48821

*Language and Cognitive Rehabilitation Computer
  Catalogue*
  Computer Learning Materials, Inc.
  P.O. Box 1325
  Ann Arbor, MI 48106

Life Sciences Associates
  1 Fenimore Road
  Bayport, NY 11705

Midwest Publications, Co.
  P.O. Box 448
  Pacific Grove, 93950

Minnesota Educational Computer Consortium
  2520 Broadway Drive
  St. Paul, MN 55513

Psychological Software Services
  P.O. Box 29205
  Indianapolis, IN 46229

Society for Visual Education, Inc.
  Department VB
  1345 Diversey Parkway
  Chicago, IL 60614

Sunburst Communications
  Room Y 7474
  39 Washington Ave.
  Pleasantville, NY 10570

*A description of some useful software is provided in Brubaker SH, Rolnick MI: *Compilation of Clinical Software for Aphasia Rehabilitation and Cognitive Retraining*. Birmingham, MI Clinical Software Resources, 1983.

Working with Families

Mary C. Kozy, A.C.S.W., and Gloria A. Tarvin, A.C.S.W.

The involvement and support of the family is vital to the outcome of rehabilitation. The relationship between individual and family identity is so strong that if one member of the family is ill or disabled the event produces considerable impact on the other family members. Research has documented that patients with interested families or those without families achieved better results than those patients with family conflicts.[1,2] Power[3] concludes that including families in the rehabilitation process can ''improve the conditions which are favorable for the process, whether recovery or productive use of residual assets.''

Our objectives in writing this unit are as follows:

- to enhance the clinician's understanding of the family as a social system
- to increase awareness of the impact of right hemisphere disorders on the family system
- to develop a two-dimensional view of the family as both our client and as our best resource
- to provide the clinician with an overview of the types of resources that can assist the family in coping at an optimal level

THE FAMILY AS A SOCIAL SYSTEM

Many theoretical frameworks have been developed and are useful in enhancing the clinician's understanding of the different influences the family can have on the patient's rehabilitation. These theories have evolved over the past 18 years and fall into three basic categories: (1) communication networks, (2) role theory, and (3) systems theory. However, it is beyond the scope of this unit to discuss family theories in depth.

Although we realize that no one theoretical framework can encompass all that is needed to work with families, we have found the systems approach to be an effective one in understanding how the family influences the adjustment of the disabled patient, how to involve the family in the treatment process, and how we can assist the family to function with a disabled family member.

In this unit, *family* is defined as an interdependent social system of two or more persons within which its members fulfill certain functions, such as promoting individualism and growth and providing a sense of belonging, security, identity, and support.

Family structures vary and represent different resources and influences on the patient. Rakel[4] outlined family structures into three areas:

1. Nuclear family—husband, wife and their children
2. Extended family—family extended to include parents and sometimes other relatives
3. Alternate family—single-parent families, landlord–tenant, unmarried adults

The family system is dynamic and complex. Systems theory maintains that stress or change in one family member impacts each family member and the group as a whole.

Under normal circumstances, the family operates as a homeostatic interdependent system. There are roles and responsibilities with division of labor. An example of role distribution is that one family member may be the primary decision maker and another may be the one who provides nurturance. Within families there are also well accepted and often unspoken values and beliefs.

According to Wiley,[5] "an optimal family structure is a system of related members whose relations may be described by lines and boundaries with each individual possessing his own thoughts, feelings, talents, skills, expectations, and dreams . . . in order for the system to endure life's challenges its structure must change; its boundaries must change."

In the presence of disability, family system functioning becomes unbalanced and upset and the system attempts to stabilize itself. For example, if the person who has a stroke was the breadwinner for the family, he may now not be able to work and provide the family income. In other words, what affects one member of an interdependent system affects the entire system. We must recognize that little in the past coping experiences of most families has prepared them to deal with a crisis of such magnitude and long duration. However, according to Regensburg,[6] "building on the patients/ families strengths and encouraging the development of their latent capacities to deal with stress-producing situations offer patients/families experiences in mastery and growth and the gratification of coping successfully."

IMPACT OF RIGHT HEMISPHERE LESIONS ON THE FAMILY SYSTEM

The effects of long-term disability are experienced not only by the patient but also by spouses, children, siblings, and others whether or not they reside in the same household.

It is our opinion that the impact of disability must be viewed from a multidimensional framework of the interrelationship of physical, psychological, emotional, social, economic, spiritual, and sexual factors (Exhibit 6–1).

Exhibit 6–1 Multidimensional Framework of the Impact of Disability on the Family

Physical:	Family members focus all their energy on the patient. They go to the hospital sometimes daily and redistribute roles at home to incorporate this change.
Psychological:	There are often feelings of guilt, with family members expressing that they should have been able to prevent the incident (e.g., "If I had made him go to the doctor, he would not have had the stroke").
Emotional:	Families may experience a range of feelings including anger, frustrations at normalization attempts, helplessness, and anxiety in trying to cope with this unique situation.
Social:	The presence of disability can cause interruptions in normal social patterns (e.g., cancellation of a vacation). Long-term disability often leads to social isolation as friends and acquaintances resume their own normal daily routines.
Economic:	Additional stress is experienced by the family around issues such as the rising costs of hospital care with decreasing insurance reimbursement rates, loss of income, and increased costs, including going to the hospital to visit the patient (e.g., parking and meals eaten in the cafeteria).
Spiritual:	It is common to hear family members asking "Why me?" and questioning God and their formerly unquestioned religious beliefs when this type of crisis occurs as they attempt to sort out and cope with the situation.
Sexual:	Sexual concerns often reflect functional and emotional loss, separation from family members while hospitalized, and role changes.

A case example will illustrate the impact of a disability on the family system:

Mr. X. was a 60-year-old physician in private practice. He lived with his wife, who had just been given a high position in a community social service agency. Their children were grown and lived out of the home. One of their daughters was a cardiac nurse. Socially active, this couple had a home in the suburbs, a good marriage, and good relationships with their children and extended family. Mr. X. suffered a right cerebrovascular accident with left hemiplegia and nondominant hemisphere syndrome. He was confined to a wheelchair, had left hemianopia and neglect, was restless and impulsive, and had questionable judgment. While Mr. X. was in the hospital, Mrs. X. started her new job; yet she tried to visit her husband every day. Their daughter was employed at a hospital near the rehabilitation center. An additional stress occurred when Mr. X.'s nephew was injured in a diving accident at Mr. X.'s summer cottage and was rendered quadriplegic.

To highlight the impact on this family system, we will briefly look at each dimensional impact.

- *Physically*—Mrs. X. was exhausted trying to learn her new job and drive to the hospital every day.
- *Psychologically*—Mr. X. was depressed and questioning his worth as a person since much of his identity was tied up in his ability to practice medicine and his roles as helper and healer.
- *Emotionally*—Mrs. X. was worried about outcome and prognosis while their daughter was experiencing a range of feelings being an "objective" nurse who understood brain damage and being a "subjective" daughter trying to understand changes in her father.
- *Socially*—This family had many friends who were concerned but lacked understanding of brain damage and expected quick recovery, which placed additional stress on the family in terms of repeatedly explaining the patient's condition.
- *Economically*—The patient's financial resources were mostly tied up in his one-man practice, and Mrs. X. knew that she had to sell the practice but that this would take time.
- *Sexually*—Mr. X.'s brain damage caused him to be more restless and impulsive and this negatively affected the couple's formerly satisfactory sexual relationship.

In viewing family systems, it is important to realize that every family system is unique. There are ethnic and other cultural considerations. Religious orientation is another major factor. Kinship networks also vary from family to family.

A disability can disrupt the balance of these factors, and the extent of the disruption depends on the life stage of the family (Exhibit 6–2).[7] A disability may occur at any one point in the developmental cycle of a family. Within each stage of the cycle there are associated tasks, problems, roles, and responsibilities. Understanding the developmental cycle of a family such as that of Mr. X. is useful in determining the family's responses and demands at a given time. It can also assist in determining the clinician's interventions. As seen in the family in the case study, the cerebrovascular accident resulted in dependency and marital problems in a previously satisfactory relationship. Attention was

Exhibit 6–2 Family Life Stages

Beginning family—married couple without children

Child-bearing family—young children

Family with preschool children

Families with school-age children

Families with teenagers

Families as launching centers (first child gone to last child leaving home)

Families in the middle years—empty nest to retirement

Aging family—retirement to death of both spouses.

Source: Power P: The utilization of the family in the rehabilitation of the chronically ill patient: Some new perspectives for the allied health professionals. *J Allied Health* 1976 (Spring):42–51.

focused almost exclusively on the patient. His daughter was required to assume a caretaking role.

There is a cardinal rule in working with families: *to start where the family is.* Several authors have described schemas of patient reactions to chronic illness, disability, and dying that lead to some form of adaptation or acceptance.[8–11] The patient's family have many of the same psychosocial problems as the patient and experience the same stages of adjustment as does the patient. They may not, and often do not, go through them in the same time frame as the patient, nor should we anticipate that every family will go through the stages as outlined. Kerr's[12] stages of adjustment to disability are a helpful way of understanding where the family might be psychologically at any given point. A pattern of reactions from shock to adjustment is described:

1. Shock. This can be a time of uncertainty, fear, confusion, and panic, as well as not knowing what to do. It is a time when psychosocial support and intervention are useful. The lack of such can result in the development of exaggerated fears and ignorance.

2. Expectancy of recovery. Our typical expectations of illness are that when a person becomes ill and goes to the hospital the illness is temporary and recovery is complete. We are not prepared for the duration and long-term stress implicit in a chronic or permanent disability. The family are operating under these expectations often when they first arrive at the rehabilitation hospital. This phase is

characterized by hope and the slow discovery of the extent of the damage and the prognosis for recovery.

3. Mourning. The family begins to recognize that life will never be exactly the same and begins to confront issues of loss, change, and rebuilding.

4. Coping. Healthy or neurotic defenses may be employed by the family in order to reestablish equilibrium in the system. This is a particularly crucial time for intervention on the part of health care professionals.

5. Adjustment. This is a period of coming to terms with the new life style. During this phase, the family reintegrates the disabled family member back into the family system's functioning. Redistribution of roles is completed. The disability and the disabled person are no longer necessarily the main focus or concern of all the family's energy.

TWO-DIMENSIONAL FAMILY PERSPECTIVE

The family can be viewed in a two-dimensional way. It is both our client and our best resource. As client the family has needs that we can help meet. Opportunities should be provided in order for family members to ventilate their concerns and have their feelings validated by us. They need support, encouragement, and feedback that they are doing a good job. It may be helpful to provide families with specific recommendations and permission to allow time for themselves and reinforcement that no one family member can care for another or be with another 24 hours a day. The family also needs our empathy. How we communicate with families should not be taken lightly. We must be careful what we communicate, both verbally and nonverbally, and pay attention to how it is perceived by the family. For example, the implications of stroke are often misinterpreted by family members, and they may tend to express anger toward the patient or react in an overly sympathetic manner.

The family is our best resource. Family members can assist us in working with a patient because of their knowledge of the patient's predisability personality and history, which can be valuable information for therapists in treating the individual. The family can provide support to the patient, can reintegrate the patient back into the family system's functioning, or if not able to care for the patient at home, can assist in locating an appropriate facility and then in acting as an advocate for the disabled person in that facility. The family can also become, in effect, adjunct-therapists, carrying out home programs with the patient. A relationship has been shown between increasing a family's knowledge level about a particular disease and subsequent improvement in self-care skills.[13]

We have found a psychoeducational approach in working with families to be useful. The family needs information in order to be able to engage in realistic planning. What we may be quick to interpret as denial on the part of the family may in reality reflect a lack of knowledge about deficits from brain damage. Families also need education around emotional reactions to disability and sometimes help in improving coping and problem-solving skills.

A family's involvement will depend on several variables, which include past relationships, learning ability, style of family functioning, and current coping and problem-solving abilities.

Families learn in many different ways. Some learn best by demonstration, others by reading, and others by hands-on experience. It is important to assess the family's learning style and provide a range of options for learning about the patient's disability and for learning to cope with the disability that is consistent with the members' learning style. For example, the family member who learns best by experience may find a therapeutic pass or home visit by the patient helpful to experience life outside the hospital. A net result may also be a chance for the rehabilitation team to get feedback from the family on problems and concerns that can possibly be resolved during the patient's stay, thus making for better preparation for discharge to the home.

Rehabilitation is a combined effort shared by the clinician, patient, and family. The team is an important concept and can be a philosophical entity as well as a concrete one, with the common goal of maximizing patient functioning. The family is an important part of this team regardless of whether or not the patient is involved in outpatient treatment, in the hospital, or in home therapies. The family is a crucial part of the team because it is often a liaison between the patient and the health care professionals. The family represents to the patient a tie to the world beyond the health care system and can ensure the carryover of treatment.

When a family member has a right hemisphere lesion, it creates many concerns, some of which are unique to this particular disability group. Most families have difficulty coping with changed behavior and personality disturbance. Uninformed family members recognize exaggerated behavior but do not often know how to interpret it. For example, they see the patient as paying less attention to his formerly impeccable appearance. They may notice impulsivity or the person being less attentive to visitors or less interested in a conversation. Family members may see signs of emotional lability, which they label as depression until they become more knowledgeable regarding brain damage deficits.

A concern of family members of stroke patients is almost always whether the person will have another stroke. When a person has a stroke it often stirs up guilt and anxiety about whether or not the stroke could have been prevented. Family members often express feeling vulnerable and lacking control. It is a natural reaction to want to regain a sense of control.

An issue often experienced by families of hemiplegic patients falls into the category of time management and time demands. Everything takes longer in terms of basic activity of daily living skills. Routines at home have to be reestablished. New skills need practice. Family members have to assume roles that were previously performed by the now disabled member. If the person has perceptual and processing problems, communicating information in an effective way also requires an extended amount of time. Energy drain on the family system may become a critical issue, such as shown in the following case study:

> Mrs. A was a 27-year-old homemaker when she had a stroke during the delivery of twins. She had been married for 4 years to a prominent businessman. Mr. and Mrs. A were an upper middle-class family whose life style reflected this socioeconomic status. Their leisure time activities centered around family, friends, and country club activities. Prior to the stroke, Mrs. A was socially active in charitable activities. She was also meticulous in her appearance and fashion conscious. Mrs. A had a right-sided cerebrovascular accident, which resulted in flat affect, denial of deficits, and altered body concept. She was totally disinterested in her children. The care of the twins required additional time demands and created a need for role redistribution. The couple's parents became involved concretely and emotionally. Mr. A assumed a greater share in parenting than had been expected. Although Mrs. A could independently perform her own self-care activities, they required additional time. Household help had to be employed for other homemaking activities such as cooking, cleaning, and babysitting.
>
> On discharge from the rehabilitation hospital, Mrs. A was ambulatory with a brace and cane. Due to cosmesis, she refused to go out of the house and become involved in any previous activities or to interact with her country club friends or anyone outside the family.

> Initially, friends visited and were involved, but they could not cope with Mrs. A's lability and depression. Visitors subsequently became less frequent, which served to reinforce Mrs. A's poor self-image. In addition, Mrs. A would not identify herself as a disabled person. Therefore involvement, for example, in a self-help group was not an option she was willing to consider.

This case study highlights another concern of the family—social isolation. When faced with a long-term disability, social networks often change and friends who visited come less frequently or not at all. This is especially true when there are behavior, personality, or cognitive deficits. Friends and acquaintances often report feeling awkward in their attempts to interact with the patient. Also, the patient may no longer be able to participate in previously satisfying social outlets and, therefore, becomes isolated from previously significant social groups. Transportation and architectural barriers are factors adding to isolation for many hemiplegics, who can no longer drive or may not have a companion-attendant to assist them out in the community. As old social networks break down, it is often more difficult for the disabled person to build new networks because of self-image and societal attitudes.

A common concern facing families in trying to reestablish equilibrium in their family system's functioning is finding the balance between helping the patient and not doing too much for the patient. The exact functional ability of the patient may be unclear to the family members, or it may be in flux. The family may have a need to treat the patient as ''normal'' and at the same time must help the person compensate for his deficits. This may be complicated by previous patterns and role divisions in the family and attitudes toward help, illness, and independence.

RESOURCES

Twenty years ago a study was conducted on mental health needs in the United States. One of the most significant findings was that persons tend to rely on their own inner resources to handle their problems. Since then, a number of researchers have attempted to plot the sources of help in a community to assist individuals in coping with their life tasks. An analysis of the sources of help falls into four resource categories: (1) self, (2) informal or natural systems, (3) formal or membership systems, and (4) societal systems.

Our goal is to help the family members mobilize inner resources in order for them to use outer resources effectively. In mobilizing resources, it is often necessary to teach families how to collect and use information. Systems negotiation is a learned skill. We instruct persons on becoming active, informed consumers.

When considering resources to aid the family, do not overlook the natural helping systems. These are the informal support networks that can serve as an extension of the family. They include extended family members such as cousins and nieces and nephews. They can include neighbors and friends. They include the church, where there are often strong bonds and established ties. The family may need assistance from us in mobilizing these systems (i.e., how to accept help and how to structure offered help).

Since illness is a tremendous economic drain on a family system, the family often needs help organizing financial resources and obtaining entitlements. Assisting the family with these practical matters can sometimes give the family direction and be the beginning of their moving out of panic or shock. Persons who are hospitalized are forced to deal with insurance systems. If they do not have insurance, they must learn to deal with public welfare systems such as Medicaid. The family must gain awareness of services and how to obtain them. If the patient who becomes disabled was employed, he may be eligible for Social Security Disability benefits. If he has not worked and has limited financial resources, he can apply for Supplemental Security Income. Both programs define disability as the inability to engage in substantial gainful employment because of physical or mental impairments. Patients may apply for these benefits through their local Social Security Administration office. If the person is a veteran and has limited income, he may be eligible for veterans' benefits, including medical services. Other entitlements vary from state to state, and these systems may be confusing, especially to the family that is already experiencing stress.

For the hemiplegic who has had a stroke, family education information can be obtained from the American Heart Association. Under the auspices of the American Heart Association are stroke clubs, which are part of the self-help group movement. Stroke clubs usually meet monthly and are educational/social groups for stroke patients and their significant others to build mutual support and engage in sharing and problem solving. For many newly disabled persons faced with rebuilding a social network, the stroke club is a good first step.

The first month home from the hospital is often the most difficult period for the patient and family. They are at a point when they are trying to cope with their altered life style and organize new routines at home. They are often anxious because they no longer have the daily support and contact with the medical caregivers. The disabled person is going through a role transition from "patient" back to "family member." For the newly disabled person leaving the hospital for the first time, home health and visiting nurse associations are a valuable community resource. These are often covered by insurance, Medicare, and Medicaid, or they may charge on a sliding scale, which makes these services accessible to most patients post discharge from the hospital. Home-care teams can provide follow-up therapies and support. They also can be a link between the hospital and the family in terms of identifying problems. Furthermore, home care teams are usually familiar with community resources and can assist the family in establishing these linkages.

In addition to assistance from nursing agencies that provide intermittent help at home, it is recommended to many families that they hire attendant caregivers. No one person can provide 24-hour-a-day help to a disabled person and effectively meet all the other role demands. With the care distributed among two or more persons, it may make it possible for the patient to receive the best care and also maintain higher quality relationships among family members. Some states have subsidized attendant care programs for persons with limited incomes. Families should be encouraged to contact local Medicaid or vocational rehabilitation departments for information about attendant care alternatives.

Transportation is one of the major resource needs of the disabled. Some towns have accessible public transportation or dial-a-ride systems. Sometimes volunteer transportation is available for medical appointments through church or civic groups such as the Red Cross.

As an alternative to hiring an attendant or to nursing home placement, many communities have instituted adult day care programs. This is a supervised activity program in which a disabled person may spend 1 or more days a week in structured activity and care while other family members are at work. It can also serve as respite care for a family trying to maintain a disabled family member at home. Such programs may be located by contacting local departments on aging, mental health centers, or churches.

For some families, emotional and psychological issues remain unresolved at the time when they leave the hospital or terminate treatment. Most communities have counseling services available through mental health or family service associations. In addition, there are private counselors who may be psychiatrists, psychologists, or social workers. Church-affiliated counseling services are also widely available, such as Catholic charities, Lutheran welfare services, or Jewish family services.

Use of time and leisure often become important issues for the disabled person who cannot resume formerly satisfying and productive life activities. Some communities have special recreation programs offered through the park district as a way of reintegrating the disabled person back into community activities. Programs offered through the regular park district may also be of interest. Community colleges and high schools in many communities have continuing education or non-credit courses. These activities not only assist with skill building but have the benefit of social interaction. For the geriatric population, senior citizen centers through towns or churches are growing in number and some of these have transportation available.

With the trend toward health and fitness, sports- and recreation-oriented clubs such as the YMCA are making their facilities more accessible to the disabled. For the person who is interested in reading as a recreational activity and because of the brain damage has become print handicapped, the Library of Congress offers a talking book program of recorded books on a library loan basis. In addition, there are approximately 100 radio information services for the print handicapped that serve to read current materials such as newspapers and magazines over a closed-circuit radio station.

For the patient who has potential to be employed, every state has a state department of vocational rehabilitation services. This agency is designed to assist the disabled in returning to gainful employment. Vocational rehabilitation services will sometimes fund equipment, schooling, work evaluation, or sheltered workshop programs for the person with vocational potential and interest.

Because resources vary from community to community and vary in eligibility criteria, it is essential for the family to become resource knowledgeable and be able to locate resources and use them independently. Families should be encouraged to keep resource notebooks. Effective communication with the resources is modeled for the family, and families are taught the assertiveness skills helpful in negotiating with systems. Resource location helpers are provided to families. These include information and referral services, which are often available through United Way agencies. Some communities have independent living centers that offer resource assistance to the disabled. The local hospital social worker is also a person who is usually familiar with resources available in the home community, as is the visiting nurse. It is suggested to families that they also receive newsletters and information from disabled consumer organizations, such as the National Head Injury Foundation, in order to receive new resource information as it becomes available.

SUMMARY

One of the primary goals of rehabilitation is to help the patient and family come to terms with the reality of the disability. This is a combined effort shared by the clinician, patient, and family. We have described emotional responses and influences that a family may have to a family member with right hemisphere lesion. We have offered strategies and resources available for the clinician's consideration in assisting the family to cope with the impact of the disability on family system's functioning.

It is important to note that there is no one way of working with all families. A range of opportunities can be provided for families to be involved and to learn. We suggest a multimedia approach to family education, drawing on written materials, specific instruction, video tapes, therapy observations, and individual meetings with team members.

Specific skills such as stress management, time management, and assertiveness training can be taught to help the families cope more effectively. However, it is not possible to work with all families. Some families have closed family systems and therefore are not accepting of outside help in solving problems.

As team members, we can model effective communication and help families identify and mobilize their natural support systems by identifying their strengths and coping resources. We can also assist the family in obtaining information about the disability that will help them understand the abilities and limitations of the disabled family member.

It is essential to remember that often our intervening with families is short term. The family had a long history previous to our involvement and will eventually resume functioning independently of us. It is our role to assist the family during the time of crisis to cope, solve problems, and learn to adapt with the least amount of stress and disruption to the family system's functioning.

Treischmann[14] believes that the key to coping with a disability is to receive enough satisfactions and rewards to make life worthwhile. If we can assist the family in believing that living with the presence of disability in the family system is worthwhile, then we have achieved the goals of rehabilitation.

REFERENCES

1. Oles ES: *Social Work Study of Aphasic Patients*. Rancho Los Amigos Hospital, Downey, California, 1966.

2. Litman TJ: The family and physical rehabilitation. *J Chronic Dis* 1966;19:211–217.

3. Power P, Dell Orto A: *Role of the Family in the Rehabilitation of the Physically Disabled*. Baltimore, University Park Press, 1980.

4. Rakel R: *Principles of Family Medicine*. Philadelphia, WB Saunders Co, 1977.

5. Wiley SD: Structural treatment approach for families in crisis. *Am J Phys Med* 1983;62:271–285.

6. Regensburg D. *Toward Education for Health Professions*. New York. Harper & Row, 1978.

7. Power P: The utilization of the family in the rehabilitation of the chronically ill patient: Some new perspectives for the allied health professionals. *J Allied Health* 1976;7:42–51.

8. Fink S: Crises and motivation: A theoretical model. *Arch Phys Med Rehabil* 1967;48:592–597.

9. Kubler-Ross E: *On Death and Dying*. New York, Macmillan, 1969.

10. Shontz F: Reactions to crises. *Volta Rev* 1965;67:364–370.

11. Weisman A: *On Death and Dying*. New York, Behavioral Publications, 1972.

12. Kerr N: Understanding the process of adjustment to disability. *J Rehabil* 1961;27:16–18.

13. Evans RL, Held S: Evaluation of family stroke education. *Int J Rehabil Res* 1984;7:47–51.

14. Treischman R: *The Psychological, Social and Vocational Adjustment to Spinal Cord Injury: A Strategy for Future Research: Final Report*. Los Angeles, Easter Seal Society of Los Angeles County, 1978.

Concluding Comments

Martha S. Burns, Ph.D.

This book represents the culmination of several years of clinical investigation into the communication problems of the patient with right hemisphere damage. As is true of much clinical research, diagnostic and therapeutic methods were inspired by the status of current theory as well as by knowledge gleaned from laboratory data. Through trial and error, techniques were developed and modified to meet the needs of individual patients.

Objective verification of the validity and reliability of the diagnostic tools presented in this book and elsewhere is a necessary next step in improving the efficacy of our approaches to evaluation. However, as is true of the treatment of other higher cognitive processes, improved methodology for the syndrome of right hemisphere damage will likely evolve as much from the cumulative clinical experiences of insightful clinicians as from the results of laboratory studies. The term *clinical insight* is used with some reservation since it is not regarded favorably in some research circles. Yet, in reality, many of the early descriptions of the pragmatic and metalinguistic impairments of the patient with right hemisphere damage came from clinical case study presentations. Surely the "split-brain," laterality, and psycholinguistic research paved the way for clinical experimentation with this population by broadening our perspective of communication on the one hand and the capacity of the right hemisphere on the other. But much of the real growth in methodology has come from

a clinical undercurrent of shared knowledge and experience. Perhaps this is as it should be, since it is, after all, the clinician who must ultimately assume responsibility for addressing the individual needs of each patient. If we have learned nothing more from the era of controlled group designs, it is that "canned treatment programs" do not withstand the test of experimental scrutiny. As skilled clinicians have recognized for some time, the therapeutic process represents a dynamic interaction between two individuals who are working together to continually reevaluate the problem and reestablish clinical objectives. Such a process does not easily lend itself to experimental manipulation.

With this admitted clinical bias in mind, we must of course still continue to look to the future for contributions from laboratory studies that can improve our understanding of the nature of right hemisphere damage as well as the rehabilitative process. At this point one can only speculate about the scientific discoveries that may impact on our field. However, some investigative avenues do provide promise for clinical direction:

Investigators working in laterality research are rapidly developing improved methods of controlling for individual processing biases that affect hemispheric processing preferences. Clear-cut dichotomies seem less viable as attentional and experiential variables are explored. As the complex interaction between hemispheric potential and individual cognitive style is more clearly delineated, clinicians will likely acquire more confidence in applying individually viable compensatory techniques that rely on intact hemispheric capabilities.

Current research using emission computed tomography of brain function will likely extend our understanding of the two hemispheres' contributions to information processing in normal individuals and after brain damage. These data should also eventually provide clinicians with insight into effective versus maladaptive therapeutic techniques.

Neurodevelopmental research at the cellular level may provide insight into the relationship between environmental stimulation and regeneration of neuronal connections. In time, such knowledge may help clinicians to coordinate intervention with the biological time clock of natural neurological recovery.

A final promising avenue of research emanates from postmortem examinations of microscopic brain cell structure. A few recent investigations of the microscopic cerebral structure of individuals with persisting developmental dyslexia have revealed regions of nonfunctional cells in territories usually specialized for language. If some developmental disturbances are eventually found to mirror neurological deficits biologically as well as functionally, clinicians may have more confidence in applying techniques proven successful with developmentally impaired populations.

In addition to the above research potential, it is likely that new horizons will evolve that neuroscience cannot even anticipate. It behooves all of us who are interested in maximizing the value of clinical intervention to remain abreast of new scientific data and to work together in application of this knowledge to the clinical milieu. One can only hope that this segment of the neurologically impaired population will not be affected by the same theoretical tunnel vision that has divided and restricted clinical growth among the aphasiological practitioners for over a century.

Index